BEYOND THE GREAT DIVIDE

101 True Stories of
Western Colorado

ABBOTT FAY

D1470529

WESTERN REFLECTIONS, INC.

Library of Congress Catalog Number:
99-60187

ISBN 1-890437-19-0

First Edition

Design and Typography by:
Patricia Wilson, Country Graphics

Published by:
Western Reflections, Inc.
P.O. Box 710
Ouray, Colorado 81427
USA

WHY BOTHER WITH THIS?

A historian said to me many years ago, "The history of Colorado has all been written; there remain only trivial details."

I believed him until I realized that in some of these so-called "trivial details" lay the true nature of what had really happened. These were the thoughts and actions of people whose opinions did not really count, but who were the architects of reality: Indians, homesteaders, miners, farmers, ranchers, businessmen and creative artisans. They made up what can truly be called the "spirit of Colorado" not the great military leaders, politicians and industrialists.

Here are the stories they remembered, not those included in the official annals of the state. These are the humorous, tragic, pathetic, sometimes horrifying moments of their lives, no matter how trivial they may have appeared to scholarly historians.

Brought together here, it is hoped that the tales represent something of the tradition of Western Colorado.

Abbott Fay
Grand Junction, Colorado
1999

TABLE OF CONTENTS

Part One
SLITHERY TRAILS AND THE DEVIL'S ELBOW

Part Two
SALUTE TO THE UTE

Part Three
SPIRITUALISTS AND SAGES

Part Four
FOUR GREAT ESCAPES

Part Five
CREATIVE COWBOYS AND STUBBORN WOMEN

Part Six
ORDEALS BY FIRE AND ICE

Part Seven
CIVILIZING THE SLOPE

Part Eight
SHAM DUELS AND OUTRAGEOUS OUTLAWS

This touring car limousine was carrying early day tourists through terrain that is typical of the "Devil's Elbow." Courtesy of Museum of Western Colorado, Research Center and Special Library

Part One

SLITHERY TRAILS AND THE DEVIL'S ELBOW

The land lying west of the Continental Divide in Colorado is replete with a variety of landforms. Elevations vary a little over 10,000 feet, from the summit of Mount Elbert to the point where the Colorado River flows into Utah. Much of the land is mountainous, with torturous trails; much of it is high plateau. Climate includes the longest growing season in the state at the Grand Valley, to the shortest, at Fraser. Precipitation totals over 500 inches a year at Wolf Creek Pass to less than eight inches at Delta. There are hot springs, deep caves, and geological freaks. The communities which grew up had their own ideas of what constituted proper behavior.

1

A CEMETERY WHICH VANISHED

Strange Burial Customs at La Posta

In English, the name of the village of La Posta means "stage station." Located about fourteen miles south of Durango on 213 Road, it was originally a stagecoach stop and post office on the route between Durango and Farmington, New Mexico. The village was established during the land rush of the Ute Strip, in which part of the Indian reservation was opened to homesteaders in May of 1899.

Most of the residents were Spanish-American, but unlike their kindred to the south, they seem to have had unique burial customs. There was, indeed, a campo santo, or burial ground, and it had been properly blessed by Father Francisco Gome. The plot was fenced off, and there was a small building in which to sing alabados, songs of praise, during the service known as the velorido, or "watch."

On the night after a person died, the corpse, wearing night clothes, was covered with cloth and brought to the outside of the cabin on a ladder. There, candles were placed on both sides of the body. If the weather permitted the mourners to be outside, a bonfire was built, coffee was drunk, and the deathwatch began. If it was inclement, the services were held indoors by candlelight.

In the morning, the body was buried, but without any casket. Dying requests were remembered: "Don't bury me in a box." There seemed to be a local horror of coffins. When there was no priest present, prayers were led by laymen; a priest would later read the funeral mass over the site.

The body was laid in the grave, in which a niche had been carved

10

where the head could rest. After the interment, no stone or marker of any sort was placed on the burial location.

There were an estimated thirty such inhumations before a chapel was built a mile away with an orthodox graveyard. In due time the property on which the earlier cemetery had existed was sold. The new owner, not realizing that it was sacred ground, plowed over the old grave yard for planting, and no one seemed to have protested. Later none seemed to remember where the burial ground had been.

Today La Posta is a mere wide spot in the road, the main highway being located on the east side of the Las Animas River from the old village.

There were others who didn't get buried in coffins — in fact they didn't get buried at all. Courtesy of P. David Smith Harper's Weekly, *April 23, 1881*

2

COLORADO'S YOUNGEST VOLCANO

It Retired Only Four Millennia Ago

On Interstate Highway I-70, at Dotsero, just east of Glenwood Canyon, one may observe many acres of rock, most visible on the south side of the highway. This is the edge of the cinder cone of the last volcano to erupt in Colorado, a massive explosion that occurred about 4,000 years ago.

The actual cinder cone is about a mile north of the highway, and has been quarried as material for cinder blocks. This point, where the Eagle River flows into the Colorado River, is replete with large boulders of the black, puffy clinkers. When the blow up took place, it may have altered the flow of the Eagle River for thirty miles upstream.

When the Denver and Rio Grande Western Railroad had completed the Moffat Tunnel beneath the Continental Divide in 1928, it connected with the Tennessee Pass Route at this point, and the popular belief is that the name Dotsero meant that this was dot zero on the railway maps. However, other sources dispute that, claiming it was a Ute word meaning "something new." Some Ute linguists deny that, claiming that it was the name of a beautiful Indian maiden who cast herself off a "lover's leap" in the area.

3

HOW TREASURE MOUNTAIN GOT ITS NAME

Asa Poor Might Have Become Rich

A few miles southwest of Wolf Creek Pass, not far from Pagosa Springs, Treasure Mountain, elevation 11,908 feet, is the location of one of Western Colorado's oldest legends of hidden gold.

There are at least a dozen stories of hidden gold or silver caches on the Western Slope, but few of them have been so persistent as the account of a group of some forty Frenchmen who came to the region about 1795 and discovered a rich lode of gold. At that time, the area, which is located within a few miles of the Continental Divide, was claimed by both Spain and France. The party had planned to spend only the summer, but the diggings proved so rich that they decided to spend the winter in Taos (now in New Mexico). The next summer even more gold was found, so they continued to mine for several years. The bonanza would be worth about forty million dollars today if tales are to be believed.

Then came trouble. Indians began to attack the miners. Some claim the natives were Utes; others say Arapahoes. Still other accounts attribute the raids to the Spaniards, who sent the Indians against the Frenchmen. In any event, the attacks were costly, and soon only a few miners were left alive. They buried the gold bullion in a tunnel set with death traps, and supposedly sealed it with a heavy door. Then they dropped the key to the door into a well.

Eventually, only one of the Frenchmen ever returned to St. Louis to tell the story. His name was Remy Ledoux.

13

By that time Napoleon had made himself emperor and had disposed of the Louisiana Territory to the United States, thus clouding any claim France might have thought it had to the San Juan Mountains. In time the hidden gold was almost forgotten.

It was not until 1842 that Ledoux's grandson studied the map his grand-pere had drawn. A group was formed to try to recover the riches. They did find a fleur-de-lis, French national symbol, sketched on a rock with an arrow beneath it. Digging all around the area, they came up empty-handed. When young Ledoux returned the next year, he apparently drowned in the Spring runoff. His body was found by another prospector, William Yule. Yule admitted many years later, while on a drinking binge, that they had taken the original map from Ledoux's body, but had never found time to make the search.

It is not known how, but eventually the map fell into the hands of one Asa Poor. Poor worked laboriously to decipher a small inscription on one corner of the map. It read "Stand on grave at the foot of the mountain at six on a September morning. Face east. Where the shadow of your head falls you'll find the gold." It is interesting that one had to face east, as in any direction the shadow would fall the same.

Poor found a grave that matched the map's account, and he discovered a sealed shaft which seemed to be a worked-out gold mine. He decided to get a group of men together to open the old mine but died before he could carry out the scheme. The map disappeared.

Since then, there have been snowslides and rockslides which have radically changed the topography of the area where the mine was supposed to have been. Some fortune hunters have tried to locate the lost lode but without success. The story was so widely believed that the mountain was given the name of Treasure. Unfortunately, it's a pretty big mountain, and who knows on which side the gold was hidden?

4

WILD WHEREABOUTS ALONG
THE WINDING DOLORES

And the Outlaw of Outlaw Mesa

As the Dolores River traverses in a meandering course through Montrose and Mesa Counties, it is surrounded by many mysterious places. It flows back and forth through Slick Rock Canyon, a labyrinth of crooked curves and torturous rapids crossing the Paradox Valley, rather than flowing down, as a river should. That's the paradox.

There is Sinbad Valley, suggestive of Arabian desertlands. Also, Wild Steer Mesa and Saucer Basin were so named long before the term U.F.O. was coined. Calamity Mesa was given that name by a prospector whose burro ate all his food supply, forcing him to go four days without anything to eat before reaching a new resource. Sewemup Mesa was where cattle rustlers cut the brands off stolen animals and sewed the hide back in place.

Then there is Outlaw Mesa. The so-called outlaw for whom it was named was in reality not an outlaw, but served the people well when he shot and killed Axel Peterson. Peterson had to be one of the most loathsome scalawags in the region. When drunk, he amused himself by shooting near the feet of school children to watch them dance. He often shot randomly at houses as he rode through the villages.

John Foster was nicknamed Pegleg. He had suffered the loss of one leg in a horrible accident at a Telluride mill. When fitted with an artificial leg, he didn't like it, and made his own out of a two-by-four. It was said he could run as fast as most anyone, and climb up steep

15

mountainsides. When Peterson started shooting at Foster's cabin one day, Pegleg's wife was almost hit. John stepped out and shot Peterson in the head, killing him instantly.

People from Norwood to Bedrock celebrated the event. In a trial at Grand Junction, there was no question that the shooting was justifiable homicide. Foster and his wife were even paid two dollars each for their testimony. Neighbors pitched in and bought Foster a new suit of clothes.

A few years later, Foster was working his uranium mine for the pitchblende which was used in early radium treatments. Another man tried to jump his claim asserting that he was there first, and called Pegleg an outlaw, referring to the earlier killing. Foster's prior claim was upheld, but the name of the uplift on which it was located never did get another moniker . . . it is still Outlaw Mesa.

5

RED CLIFF'S MAGNIFICENT "CRYSTAL CAVE"

Complete with an Underground Ship!

There have been a number of stories about underground caverns discovered by hard rock miners in the West. The most fantastic of these must have been the one near the town of Red Cliff. Red Cliff, in the deep canyon of the Eagle River west of Tennessee Pass, was undergoing a mining boom in 1879. Fabulous stories about mineral wealth there were circulated in Colorado and to potential Eastern investors.

It seems that Jacob Cahee and Louis Adams came into the town and told of a marvelous crystal cave they had found. The two men were sinking a shaft at the base of a nearby mountain. They were digging in loose surface gravel when they struck a layer of limestone. As they began to hack through it, the rock gave way beneath their feet.

Suddenly they were in a cavern 240 feet long and 180 feet wide, sparkling with crystals of quartz interlaced with gleaming gold! To their amazed eyes appeared a sailing ship made of dark and porous wood, like walnut. The ends of the vessel turned up "like the toe of a Moorish slipper." The deck was held in place with nails of "hard copper." Twenty-foot masts with shreds of sails bedecked the ship. It had a gold instrument that looked like a sextant, and there were decorations on the side which appeared to be Chinese characters.

This must have been the ship of some ancient civilization which had sunk when the limestone was being formed! Very few people at that time knew anything about the science of geological formations, or the story would have been laughed out of existence. It was, instead, taken at face value and published in newspapers in Leadville and Denver. Authors McDonald Knight and Leonard Hammond, in *Early Days on the Eagle*, suggest that the editors may have had "tongue in cheek" in publishing these stories.

In a scrapbook found in Leadville there was a large line engraving of the magnificent cavern with its ship, taken from a national publication which, unfortunately, was not identified, so the story received credence outside of Colorado. Indeed, the story was still told in those parts as late as the 1950s, seventy years after the publication. Newcomers were told of the great cavern, and a few prospectors hoped to find the site which had somehow been lost after the story appeared in 1880.

6

THOSE CRAMPED AND SLITHERY TRAILS

Tailing the Burro

Some Western Colorado highways are considered a bit scary by drivers who are not familiar with them. There is the west side of Independence Pass, a shelf ledge above the Aspen area, which is still quite narrow.

Perhaps the most recognized is the narrow shelf on Red Mountain Pass, the so-called "Million Dollar Highway." Back in the days when most service stations were full-service a popular joke related that motorists who had crossed the pass and arrived in Ouray or Silverton would pull into a station, and the attendant would come out and inquire, "Gas, oil, unstick your hands from the steering wheel?" That road is a regular boulevard today, compared to a few decades ago. When Otto Mears, "Pathfinder of the San Juan" first carved the route, it was barely wide enough for a single wagon to get by, with very few passing lanes.

That part of the state is notorious for avalanches, in addition to the treacherous roads. When J. J. Gibbons, a priest, was serving Ouray, Silverton and Telluride, he had many close calls in his commutes. When crossing Imogene Pass from Ouray to Telluride, he realized that there was still snow on parts of the trail. He looked off the edge of the steep slope and saw several dead horses at the bottom, commenting, "At the time I had never thought of horses falling and rolling a quarter of a mile over rocks." When his own horse fell to his knees several times, Gibbon realized the horseshoes were old and worn. He got off and led the horse through the icy rock-strewn path. Coming from the other side another rider asked about the trail, and Gibbon told him it was no good unless his horse was properly shod.

19

So the stranger got off and led the horse, but the priest was horrified to see the horse slide off to his doom and join the carcasses below.

When snow was very deep, burros were often more sure-footed than the miners who drove them. On steep passages the men would hang on to the tail of the burro to have some stability, a practice known as "tailing."

While there was no snow, one prospector decided to be kind to his two pack animals. William Mark was crossing the Continental Divide over the shoulder of Mount Massive in 1880. He reached the narrow ledge of a trail above the West Frying Pan River, where he found "steep rock-steps two feet and more high, crevices in which there is hardly room enough for a horse's hoof." This was at a point which was known as "Devil's Gate." He remarked that most travelers at the point take the loads on their own shoulders, as he did, "As they, in case of a slip, can throw the load off, which an animal could not do." Eventually, this would be the route of the Colorado Midland Railroad which crossed beneath the divide in the Busk-Ivanhoe Tunnel.

This miner is following the tradition of "tailing the burro" in deep snow.
Photo Courtesy of P. David Smith

7

GAMBLING AND DANCING FOR GOD

A Tale of Two Cities

It was an unusual pair of men who showed up in Rico one day in 1880. Parson Hogue, a Man of the Cloth seeking to found a church, was a close friend of Brownie Lee, a professional gambler. Rico was just getting started as a mining boom town and had numerous saloons and gambling houses, but the largest structure was a big dance hall.

Brownie went around during the week and told all the folks in the bars that the games should close down for an hour the following Sunday "to give the parson a chance to deal" in the big hall.

Sunday morning there were many gamblers going strong in the assigned place at the sacred hour. However, they all stopped and listened as Parson Hogue gave an impassioned sermon. Hymnals were distributed, and the crowd enjoyed spirited singing in praise of the Lord. As soon as the service ended, Lee stood up and asked for a collection so that a church could be built, thus not interfering with the gambling on Sunday mornings.

He said it was a "four-bit ante game, table stakes, no limit" and got a fine donation from the crowd. This was believed to be the first religious service in Rico.

About that same period in history two of the most famous palaces of entertainment in West Gunnison were the Red Light Dance Hall and Fat Jack's Saloon. At the latter establishment, there was a tradition that on Sunday evenings the Sabbath was observed by having the orchestra play only sacred music.

According to a participant, George A. Root, the dancing went on, and "it was by no means an uncommon sight to see sundry couples

21

cavorting about the floor." The ladies were "bedecked and bespangled in brief and extravagantly decollete dresses" with their sturdy companions garbed in miners' costumes and each with a brace of six-guns strapped to his hip.

The couples "tripped the light fantastic" to such hymns as "Jesus, Lover of My Soul" or "The Beautiful Gates Ajar." Other hymns brought forth the rhythm for square dances. Root added that the refreshments served at these hours were of the "lighter sort."

Colorado gambling halls were seedy affairs. Almost any game of chance could be found here. Frank Leslie's Newspaper 4/26/1879 *Courtesy of P. David Smith*

8

ELEPHANTS CROSSING THE ROCKIES

The Little Train That Couldn't Quite Make It

Boreas Pass, between the South Park town of Como and the then-booming mining town of Breckenridge, was the highest railroad crossing in the world in 1883. The pass, named for the Greek god of the North Wind, was well-named, being swept by numerous storms at its 11,498 foot summit.

Grades were so steep on both sides of this Continental Divide pass that narrow-gauge trains of the Denver and South Park Railroad's "High Line" were limited to only three cars.

When P.T. Barnum's circus scheduled a performance in Breckenridge, at least two sections of train were needed. When the train carrying the menagerie neared the top of the pass, it gradually stalled with the weight. The lions and tigers were getting restless, and the handlers did not know how to handle them in the thin, frigid air.

It was then decided to remove the elephants and press them into service, pushing the train from behind until it crossed the summit to the Western Slope. It could be, of course, that simply removing the elephants may have reduced the weight enough to let the little locomotive get over on its own, but this made a better story.

According to historian Perry Eberhart, "The European Alps had Hannibal and his elephants. Colorado had Barnum and his elephants on Boreas Pass."

23

9

CURIOUS STOPS ON THE ROARING FORK LINE

Mary Got to Go All the Way to Aspen

Back in the days when railroads had many stops for now long-forgotten communities, the railroad from Glenwood Springs to Aspen had some with given names of people. These included: Leon, Rathbone, Emma, Woody, Watson and Catherine.

In his history of the Roaring Fork Valley, the route of the railroad, Len Shoemaker told stories which conductors on the trains swore were true.

Soon after leaving Carbondale, the conductor came into the passenger car and called out "Catherine!" As the train came to a stop, a woman got off. A little later, the cry was for "Emma!" Another lady left the train there. Closer to Aspen, the trainman called out, "Woody!" and a man left from the car.

As the conductor left to go into the next car, a woman, visibly disturbed, came up to him and said, "My name is Mary, but I want you to know I'm going to Aspen and I'll not leave this train until it gets there!" As the conductor thought about it, he was able to reassure her that he felt the engineer could now pull the remaining passengers safely into town.

On another occasion, the train headed for Glenwood was stopped as a mudslide covered the roadbed. After investigating, the conductor informed the passengers they would probably have to spend the entire night on the train as it would take that long to clear the rails. One man found he could not accept that fate and began to rant about the poor service. In trying to calm him, the trainman commented, "Why, man, you ought to consider yourself lucky. Few men have the chance of sleeping between Emma and Catherine, as you have. Why don't you take advantage of it?"

10

THE MONSTER WHO DEVOURED WEST BRECKENRIDGE

Royal Tiger's Gold-Hungry Dredge

Breckenridge had always been a rich source for hydraulic mining, in which water pressure is used to wash the precious gold from the sides of the mountains. By the beginning of the twentieth century, there were already ugly pits along the Blue River, but what gold was left was too deep and covered with many huge boulders making that type of mining unprofitable.

It was then that the dredge showed up. It was a gigantic factory three stories high which created the very pond upon which it floated, moving the pond forward as it gulped up the gigantic rocks and left them behind. A huge arm extended in front to dig up the meadows and trees. After the gold had been taken from the stream bed, another great arm dumped the refuse behind. Gradually, moving back and forth across the valley, the machine cut a swath a hundred yards wide and eighty feet deep. In place of the beautiful river, there was nothing but "boulder trails" often fifty feet in height.

Starting in 1914 the Tonopah Placers Company had recovered nearly 150,000 ounces of gold and more than 36,000 ounces of silver by 1923. As the monster had started two miles below the town of Breckenridge, it moved upstream, bringing its owners more than three million dollars in gross revenue.

By 1922, the huge dredge had reached the city limits of Breckenridge. Many people in the town cried that "enough is enough," although others felt that the employment it brought the town was worth much more than scenic beauty. Town leaders decided that the dredge could not come into the town, and by that time Tonopah was losing money, so it abandoned the operation. The dredge was later sold to the Royal Tiger Mines Company.

In the showdown of the 1920s, Tiger threatened to continue down the main street of the town.

Then came the Great Depression and unemployment. Anxious to do something about the hard times, the town board allowed the dredge to start up once more, and proceed through the western part of town to Watson Avenue in 1932. With its frightful noise of tumbling stone, the behemoth gobbled up the narrow-gauge railroad depot and residences, as well as a park. When the World War II War Production Board demanded that gold mining in Colorado be ceased to release manpower and machinery to more demanding uses, the dredge came to rest at Jefferson Avenue and was never used again.

Two famous ladies wrote nationally popular literature which dealt with this environmental disaster. They lived together on French Street. Belle Turnbull wrote a dramatic prose poem, "Goldboat," which described the agony of destruction. Her roommate, Helen Rich, described a fictional town (obviously Breckenridge) in her novel, *The Willow Bender*. The novel tells of the restlessness of people in the little mountain valley, awaiting that inevitable last heavy storm of spring. It describes the shock when they realize the dredge is going to take their homes.

As of this writing, Breckenridge has become a popular ski resort with a music institute for summer attraction. At tremendous expense of energy and money, some of those ugly boulders have been covered or removed, and now a lovely park exists along the restored river where once the dredge loomed so large. Downstream the rocky remains still show the deluge where the lust for gold tore up the valley.

11

NEGOTIATIONS AT THE DEVIL'S ELBOW

When the Limousine Met the Jalopy

Today it is something of a boulevard compared to the narrow road of the 1930s. This is known as the "Trough Road," a mostly unpaved but well-graveled route between the towns of State Bridge and Kremmling. The drive is designated as one of Colorado's "Scenic and Historic Byways."

In the earlier days the downhill automobile had to back up to a wider spot in order to allow an oncoming upward-bound vehicle to pass. At one spot on that road there is a reverse turn which overlooks the awesome Gore Canyon, many hundreds of feet below. The Colorado River roars along beneath a steep drop-off at this place, known as the "Devil's Elbow."

Maneuvering a limousine over this road was a great challenge, but someone hadn't explained that to the wealthy driver whose hands were frozen to the steering wheel as he rounded the elbow and started down toward State Bridge. To his horror he met another car, an older model, coming up to meet him.

No way was the aristocrat going to try to back up that long car to the elbow! He stopped, got out of his Cadillac and confronted the owner of the flivver. The latter man explained that if he backed up, he wouldn't be able to get started again on the steep grade.

At last the affluent owner asked the driver of the jalopy what his crate was worth. The cost came to a hundred dollars. Thereupon the man was offered that amount and the cost of a bus ticket to his destination from State Bridge. After personal items were removed, the fated auto was gently nudged over the cliff to the chasm below, and its former owner was honored to drive the limousine on down to the bus stop.

12

A SHOCKING EVENT ON ELECTRIC PASS

Highly-Charged "St. Elmo's Fire"

Mountaineers above timberline sometimes experience a frightening phenomenon known as "St. Elmo's Fire." Perhaps in handing a sandwich to a friend, blue sparks encircle the meeting hands; at other times the current jumps between two climbers. It is often enough to cause the climbers to decide the summit is not worth reaching, and to retreat to the woodlands below.

As described by scientists, St. Elmo's fire is an ionization process, also known as "point discharge" or "corona discharge", whereby the accumulation of positive charge at elevated points, because of the attraction of negative charge on storm clouds, create an intense electrical field. The name came from the patron saint of sailors. Seamen saw wreaths of blue light at the top of masts before an impending electrical storm and regarded them as an omen of danger. St. Elmo's fire has also been seen emanating from the topmost points of church steeples.

Usually, the sparks are harmless, sort of superannuated form of static electricity which many people experience walking over a carpet on dry days. The earliest mention of strong currents is recorded by members of the Hayden Survey of 1873-75 near what came to be named Hayden Peak in Pitkin County. It is located above the town of Ashcroft.

Beneath that peak is a pass 13,200 feet in elevation. It was there, in the early 1920s, that forest ranger Len Shoemaker was building a trail to Conundrum Hot Springs. Suddenly he encountered static electricity powerful enough to knock him down three times. After the third impact, he ran his hand through his hair and got "handfuls of live sparks." Afraid to stand up, he rolled over and over down the slope until reaching a safer zone. He decided then and there to name this place Electric Pass.

Shoemaker set up a camp, but was ill all night, and then, returning to Aspen, he spent three days in bed before going back to work.

He applied to the authorities, and they approved the name of Electric Pass, and also named another nearby mountain Electric Peak.

There is also an Electric Mountain in Delta County which probably had a similar reason for its name, but there is no documented experience such as that of Len Shoemaker.

A surveying party has surprised a band of Rocky Mountain Sheep in this early (and exaggerated) drawing. Courtesy of P. David Smith Frank Leslie's Popular Magazine

13

HIGHEST FORT IN NORTH AMERICA

A Very Cold Winter on Imogene Pass

In the autumn months of 1903, the mines at Telluride were subjected to a massive labor strike which soon became violent. On November 20, in response to the demands of mine owners, Governor James H. Peabody ordered the state militia into the mining town. The troops arrived on a special train four days later, and were described as mostly young men—"just kids." It was very exciting for the young troopers, especially when they could escort union agitators and many other striking miners to a train to Montrose, to inform them that they could not return.

Despite that warning, several strikers tried to come back on the railroad but were dispatched on the next returning train. There was, however, another route into Telluride. It was over Imogene Pass, slightly higher than 13,000 feet above sea level. Well over timberline, this precarious route was usually closed during the winter months. Only a lonely shack stood atop the road to house a maintenance man for the power line that crossed the gap. The only method of transportation was by skis or snowshoes.

Some of the outcasts were determined to return to the town in which martial law had been declared. By January no one was permitted on the streets of Telluride after 8:00 P.M. without a special pass. A few of the evicted miners undertook the arduous journey from Ouray over the pass and reached the town.

It was then that the state militia established what came to be called "Fort Peabody." It was nothing more than a tiny shack surrounded by a wall fashioned from the rocks which dominated the landscape, exposed to the wind and since it was located at the very highest levels, relatively free of snow. The temperature rarely climbed as high as zero during the two months that the soldiers were stationed there.

Whether they stopped any miners was never recorded. At least the power lineman had some company, with the fort only a few hundred feet away.

Remains of this fort may still be seen above the pass itself, reached only by four-wheel drive vehicle, horse, or walking shank's mare today.

That little bump way up on the top of the mountain to the left is Fort Peabody. Courtesy of P. David Smith

14

MIRACLES AT THE MOUNT OF THE HOLY CROSS

Soggy Handkerchiefs from the Bowl of Tears

In 1928, the *Denver Post* sponsored a pilgrimage to Mount of the Holy Cross, elevation 14,005 feet, which is south of the town of Minturn. A minister believed that those who suffered from various ailments might find a cure if they had the courage and faith to ascend nearby Notch Mountain for a spectacular view of a snow-filled cross which gave the peak its name.

There, a prayer service was held, and several pilgrims reported miraculous healing. Later that year, an elderly invalid woman was brought to the site by a treacherous wagon and horse trek and reportedly walked down on her own legs which had been totally useless for years.

When a clergyman in Denver suggested that ailing supplicants mail their handkerchiefs to him to be carried to Notch Mountain, over a hundred people responded. The pastor prayed over the bits of cloth, and returned them to their owners. Again came the reports of mystic healings.

By 1932, more than two thousand people nationwide had sent personal items for the blessing. By that time, President Hoover had declared the Mount of the Holy Cross to be a National Monument.

Beneath the towering pinnacle, there is a small lake, appropriately named The Bowl of Tears. Soon radio ministries were promoting the idea of the handkerchiefs being sent to be dipped in these "holy waters." Response was overwhelming, and park rangers had to use pack mules to carry the water-soaked cloths down the trails.

By 1938, the enthusiasm had declined, and there were no more organized pilgrimages to the viewing site or the Bowl of Tears. When the United States entered World War II, the region was included in the reservation of Camp Hale, training site for the famed Tenth Mountain Division of ski and mountaineering troops.

Thousands of pastcards, similar to this one, were sent out from the Mount of the Holy Cross. Courtesy of P. David Smith

Sometime during those years, the right arm of the famous junction of crevasses was subject to rockslides which partially ruined the effect of the famous cross, whose photograph had graced many thousands of homes. It was then dropped from the listing of National Monuments.

More details on the history of that site are to be found in Robert L. Brown's *Holy Cross: The Mountain and the City.*

15

MAYBELL'S OLD VICTORY HOTEL

Does a Friendly Ghost Live There?

Among the fascinating old hotels that are still in operation in Western Colorado, the Victory in Maybell may have had some of the most interesting visitors.

This was the jumping-off place for the notorious outlaw land of Brown's Hole, where the Green River dips into the northwest corner of Colorado and departs through the Gates of Ladore into what is now Dinosaur National Monument.

The hostelry got its name for U.S. Highway 40 which was named Victory Way following the first World War. Built at the end of that conflict in 1918, the inn became a popular stop on the long coast-to-coast route, which was the preferred highway until displaced by Interstate 80 across Wyoming.

Most of the construction material was reclaimed from a defunct flour mill. With eleven sleeping rooms and two baths, this was a favorite stopping place for many cowboys who still rode horses to places such as Meeker and Elk Springs. When the automobile era arrived, there were many winter nights when the new highway was closed, giving the hotel a full house.

With its late Edwardian furnishings, the frame structure played host to many hunters who flocked to the famous elk and deer herds that abound in that region. One of its owners over the years was Tony "Deadeye" Kathrein, who was considered one of the best guides in the Rockies.

Scores of uranium prospectors made the hotel their headquarters during the exciting days of the 1950s when latter-day Argonauts jeeped all over the isolated region with their Geiger counters hoping

As shown in this photograph The Victory Hotel was called the Evans House prior to the end of World War I. Courtesy of Dave Wooden

to find radioactive minerals. There were also government representatives for land, wildlife, and mining surveys who found themselves too far away to return to their homes at night.

At this writing, the hotel still operates, owned by Ruby Wooden, and operated by Dave and Oneta Wooden. Ruby reports that the hotel is also occupied by a "friendly ghost" who walks up and down the stairs late at night when there is no one lodged upstairs.

16

THE MIRACULOUS PINES OF SILVERTON

Flourishing on the Steep, Crusty Mountainside

Overlooking the town of Silverton, on the bleak, steep slope of Anvil Mountain, is a gracefully arched shrine with a large marble statue of Christ. It is more visibly enhanced by a small forest of Scotch pines, the only trees on the slope.

In the 1950s, Silverton was suffering a severe depression. All the mines had closed, and there was no other real income for the town. It was then that the local Catholic Men's Club decided to build the shrine. Native rock was brought up to the site, which was donated by San Juan County, and a tasteful alcove was constructed. People made donations for a $5,000 statue of Italian marble to be the centerpiece of the shrine. The statue, weighing twenty tons, was hoisted into position.

The result was beautiful. Also, some said it was a miracle when a mining company reopened, putting men to work again. There was only one shortcoming. The shrine did not stand out from the barren, rock-strewn background.

It was then that Father Joseph P. McGuinness decided that the effect would be much better if the shrine was backed by trees. He was told that if God wanted trees on that lower half of the mountain, they would already be there. Foresters pointed out that the trees the priest had in mind, Scotch pines, did not grow in that soil, if such the crusty earth might be called.

McGuinness was not to be deterred, and ordered a thousand seedlings. Workers planted them behind the structure, and watered each tiny sapling for several weeks to give them a good start. Then came the second miracle. The pines grew to make a graceful background for the shrine.

In 1978, a disaster occurred at the Sunnyside Mine, when Lake Emma, 12,000 feet above sea level, broke over the mine and flooded it completely. It was a Sunday, and no one was in the mine. This was considered another miracle which some attribute to the shrine.

Silverton is snuggled in the valley. The shrine is halfway up the hill at the left. Courtesy of P. David Smith

17

FORT LEWIS HAD SEVERAL LIVES

Military, Educational and Bovine Disciplines

Today, Fort Lewis, a few miles south of the town of Hesperus, is a research center operated by Colorado State University. Much of the study there centers on the breeding and rearing of bulls. In addition to the barns and pens, there are a few well-constructed brick buildings which hark back to the days of more dramatic and colorful events at that site.

The original fort was established in 1881 to supervise the removal of the Ute Indians to their assigned reservations. In that area, the lines of the Southern Ute Reservation adjoined a number of ranches settled by whites. In as much as the Indians did not read maps, nor care much, there were a number of alarmed homesteaders who feared the Utes would attack. The Utes had the right to hunt out of the boundaries, and sometimes, when the game was scarce, a rancher's cow would do just as well. With numerous disputes, the troopers at Fort Lewis were kept busy for a decade. In 1891, there seemed to be relative peace so the military relinquished control of the site to the Bureau of Indian Affairs.

That agency established Fort Lewis as a school in which to teach Ute children the elements of reading, writing and farming. The superintendent realized that Ute names were almost impossible to pronounce, much less spell. It was thus decided that the students, all boys, should choose names which could be adapted from the history texts. It was for this reason that the Indian School was the place where such luminaries as Thomas Jefferson, John Adams, Ulysses Grant and Andrew Jackson received their educations. Chester A. Arthur was the brother of Abraham Lincoln. Lincoln, incidentally, later became a noted silversmith and a popular singer at Fort Defiance, Arizona.

By 1910 the Bureau gave up trying to make Ute children into farmers, having met with only minimal success. Ft. Lewis and its corresponding Teller Institute in Grand Junction were discontinued. The property was then turned over to the state of Colorado. Colorado A and M College made it into a vocationally-oriented high school. Students who were admitted from all walks of life had to have proof of high character and habits.

In 1927, beginning college level courses were added; and in 1933, Fort Lewis became a junior college which attracted students from throughout the La Plata County region. As more and more students arrived from Durango, it was decided in 1956 to move the college, now a four-year institution, to Durango. There a beautiful campus overlooking the city was established. It was no longer a branch of what had then become Colorado State University, but was still governed by the State Board of Agriculture.

As of this writing, the college is a thriving institution of higher learning. It is the only college in Colorado which admits qualified Native American students without charging a tuition fee, thus retaining some of its earlier tradition.

Utes play baseball at the Ute Indian School at Ft. Lewis about 1920. Courtesy of P. David Smith

These typical Utes are shown in Durango about the turn of the century. Courtesy of P. David Smith

Part Two

A SALUTE TO THE UTE

There were seven bands of Utes, five in what is now Colorado, when explorers of European descent discovered their lands in Western Colorado. No more than 5,000 Indians lived there, and they were not even unified in spoken dialects.

They would be pushed to reservations by the acquisitive miners, ranchers and farmers, but they never did give up. Many kept fighting long after the expulsion from their hunting and gathering mountain lands. They did not give in to efforts to "Americanize" the Native Americans. Their pride in their customs and traditions has never diminished in spite of the short shrift they are given in modern history.

18

HOW THE UTES VIEW CREATION

And Their Last Brave Stand

Archeologists and anthropologists often disagree about when the Utes first appeared in what is now Colorado. Some artifacts that are distinctly Ute date back to about 1400 A.D., but there seems to be little evidence of such a culture prior to that time.

In the Ute belief, these people were always here. The following is the official Ute Creation Story:

Once there were no people in the world. Sinawaf, the Creator, began to cut sticks and place them in a large bag. Coyote watched him. This went on for a long time, until Coyote's curiosity could not stand the suspense any more.

One day while Sinawaf was away, Coyote opened up the bag. Many people came out, all speaking different languages, and scattering in every direction.

When Sinawaf returned, there were but a few people left in the bag. He was very angry with Coyote, for Sinawaf planned to distribute the people equally on the land. The result of the unequal distribution caused by Coyote would be war between the different people of the world, each trying to gain land from his neighbor.

Of the people remaining in the bag, Sinawaf said, "This small tribe shall be known as the Nooch (Ute). They will be very brave and able to defeat the rest. I will place them high in the mountains, so they will be close to me."

More recent studies have suggested that there are some similarities between the rock art of the prehistoric Fremont culture in Colorado and Utah and that of the "modern" Utes. This has given

42

rise to an idea of much older habitation by what are now the Utes. However, the Utes of today are adamant in their statements: "We did not migrate from somewhere. We have always been here. We are not Fremont or Anasazi. We are Nooch."

In 1870 a Piute Indian had a revelation that the world would be subjected to a great flood, destroying all humanity. Only the Indians would be resurrected to rule the earth as they had before. When he died, his son, Wovoka, introduced the Ghost Dance, and its belief that the prophecy would be fulfilled. Many tribes, including some of the Utes, were taken up with the belief, declaring Wovoka as a Messiah. This led to uprisings against the whites, the most horrifying result being the massacre of the Sioux at Wounded Knee.

Shortly after the beginning of the twentieth century, President Theodore Roosevelt authorized taking some of the Ute reservation for national forests, and allowing homesteading on other areas. A new generation, feeling their fathers had been betrayed long enough, sought to join the Sioux, who also had a large contingency of young rebels. The idea was to attack the whites and take back their legacy.

Some 300 Utes set out for South Dakota. When they reached the Sioux, the insurgents realized the hopelessness of their quest. They were destitute and hungry. The United States Army took them as prisoners of war. They were provided with clothing, food, and transportation back to the Uintah Reservation in Utah. The last of them returned in 1908. The cost of the supplies and transport was charged against the annuities which had been allocated to the tribe.

This pathetic attempt at defiance was the last recorded declaration of war against whites by any of the United States tribes.

19

THE DIRE PROPHECY OF SPIQUET PAH

Why There Are Hot Sulphur Springs

Williiam N. Byers, founder of the *Rocky Mountain News*, was also the developer of a resort known as Hot Sulphur Springs. He made friends with the Ute Indians of the region in the 1860s and led several expeditions of exploration to that region, including John Wesley Powell's search for a good route to the Colorado River.

Byers related a number of folk tales of the Utes; one related to the founding of the springs themselves.

It seems that long ago there were many Utes, and they enjoyed the bounties of Middle Park and its plentiful game, living in peace and harmony for as many years as there are hairs upon the head. However, a young brave began to yearn for more. He longed for an attack on the Sioux, down on the plains, where the men would return with much wealth and many captives.

An old medicine man, Spiquet Pah (Smoking Water) was very upset at the talk of war. Nevertheless, many of the men were tantalized by the thought of glory and the excitement of an attack.

Spiquet Pah spoke before a council meeting on what the Utes called the "Great Plain", or Middle Park. He warned that such war-like actions would bring devastation to the tribe. He cautioned, "As the North Wind soon brings the snows and death of winter, so would he bring sorrow and death to our people . . . . If you do this, strength and peace and plenty will depart from us forever. Health will be for but few; joy will be seen no more."

It was the autumn of the year, and rather than go out to hunt, most of the men, shaming their companions as cowards, followed the brave into combat with the plains people. The Utes were soundly defeated, with many Ute scalps hanging in Sioux lodges and some of the younger boys being taken as slaves.

As they left, the old man, realizing what would happen, went to the heart of the mountain, and "pulled the hole in after him." He sat on his haunches beside his subterranean fire, which heated the water as it passed in its underground stream.

His prophecy became true. Starvation and disease followed, and there were few young men to hunt needed food and other supplies each year. The springs still flow, a warm reminder of their rash behavior.

Indian medicine men work their magic over a patient.
Courtesy of P. David Smith Harper's Weekly, *June*
20, 1868

20

PLACING A CURSE WITH A CAMERA

William H. Jackson and the Ute Women

Unquestionably, the most famous of the early photographers in Colorado was William H. Jackson. He was the first to get the Mount of the Holy Cross on film and prove such an inspirational natural Christian symbol really existed.

Traveling as the official cameraman of the Hayden Survey in 1873 and 1874, Jackson visited the original Los Pinos Ute Indian Agency in May of the latter year. This agency was then about twenty miles west of Cochetopa Pass. (It would later be transferred to the upper Uncompahgre Valley.)

In the entourage was Ernest Ingersoll, a naturalist and correspondent for the *New York Tribune*, who witnessed the problems of getting good photos of the Native Americans.

On approaching the Ute Camp near the agency, Jackson was able to get some good distance shots of the tepees. After entering the camp, he was able to locate Ouray, the spokesman for the Uncompahgre Utes who was awaiting distribution of United States Government food allotments. Ouray served as interpreter, and agreed to have his picture taken.

According to Ingersoll, Ouray bedecked himself in the manner of a true chief, and agreed that his beautiful wife, Chipeta, might also be photographed. She dressed in a fine outfit but was reluctant to pose until persuaded by a Mr. Bond, the Indian Agent.

It was the next day, though, that trouble ensued. Jackson had a visit with Peah, another leader who spoke a little English and Spanish. Peah conceded that it might be all right for Jackson to take individual pictures of some of the men, but was never to aim the camera at any woman or papoose. It would, Peah declared, cause them to become sick and perhaps even die. Others of the men would also not allow themselves to be exposed to the killer camera. They further forbade any photos of their horses.

They felt so strongly about this matter that when Jackson was ready to take a picture of two men in the cookhouse, a horse rider came up to the open doorway and threw a blanket over both photographer and camera. Jackson came out from under the blanket and saw there were several other horsemen standing by to reinforce the action.

Thus, both Jackson and Ingersoll spent the rest of the day watching the Utes, visiting with some, but packing the camera equipment away for that visit.

This is the photo of Peah (on the left) which was taken before the Utes decided the camera would make them sick. Courtesy of P. David Smith

21

FIGHTING BRAVES DRIVEN OVER THE EDGE

Cornered on Battle Rock

While it is generally considered to be a Ute Indian legend, there is some historical evidence that the horrible battle that allegedly took place on Battle Rock actually occurred. It overlooks McElmo Canyon, west of the city of Cortez in Montezuma County.

The rock itself has a huge sloping plane on top and extends over the canyon some eighty to a hundred feet above the canyon floor. Two opposing tribes of Indians, probably Navajo and Ute, were in combat nearby. It is not known which group of warriors was winning the conflict, but the other braves were driven back to take refuge on the rock, believing the battle over.

Then came the onslaught. The winning tribe drove the braves on the rock back to the edge, killing some who did not prove to be strong enough to defend themselves. The survivors finally were driven to the rim, where still fighting, they were forced over the brink, falling to their deaths at the bottom of McElmo Canyon.

The site was thereafter named Battle Rock in the Ute language. This was not a case of mass suicide; it was probably a story of poor tactical judgment and heroic struggle for survival.

22

WHY IGNACIO LEFT IGNACIO

Can Mother Earth Be Owned?

In 1880, a dying Ouray, spokesman for the Uncompahgre Utes, who had been regarded as "Chief" of all Utes, was coerced into signing the so-called "Washington Treaty." It relinquished all Ute lands in Colorado except for a strip a hundred miles long and fifteen miles wide along the New Mexico border to the Utah line.

Not consulted were the three bands of Utes relegated to this reservation. These were the Mouche and Capotes, who were mostly living in New Mexico, and the larger Weminuche band, which populated the southern San Juan Mountains. These people were promised the land with "absolute and undisturbed use and occupation" for all time.

The Mouche and Capote bands had been dealing with whites in the form of the Spanish and later Americans for centuries, and perhaps understood the idea of personal land ownership. The Weminuche, on the other hand, never could understand that any human could "own" Mother Earth.

The headquarters for this new reservation was named for Ignacio, chief spokesman for the Weminuche. It was intended as a compliment to him, and perhaps as an attempt to gain his cooperation as designated leader of all the Southern Utes.

Under the "agreement," Indians were each given two dollars to represent the sale of the land they had left. Then they were to receive individual property rights within the reservation. This was a ploy to divide the natives into separate loyalties rather than to remain in clans. Ignacio could not stand this idea. Finally, in 1895, he led his tribe west and settled in Mancos Canyon. He would not have a system of individual ownership . . . the land would belong to the tribe as a whole. This is how the mountain Utes had always lived.

No longer having the army unit at Fort Lewis to enforce obedience, the United States Government conceded the issue, and set up a new post south of the town of Mancos, thus splitting the designated lands into Southern Ute and Ute Mountain Utes, Ignacio's people. In 1915, the headquarters was moved to Towaoc (pronounced Tow-Yok) beneath the Sleeping Ute Mountain near the Utah border. The Ute Mountain Utes would own the land in common.

As Ignacio had feared, the individual owners of land in the former reservation were sometimes unable to farm it, as the government intended, and some sold their allotment to white settlers, thus creating a patchwork pattern on part of the reservation. Later there were other intrusions. An unoccupied "Ute Strip" was opened along part of the New Mexico border for homesteading; mining claims were exempted from Ute control, and eventually Mesa Verde National Park took a large segment of the reservation land.

Despite some outstanding exceptions, most attempts to turn Utes into farmers were doomed to failure. It was characteristic of the time that white policy was that if Indians anywhere could only be made into farmers and Christians, they would enjoy the same favor of God which had brought success to the people of the United States.

23

TABERNASH AND BILLY COZENS

The Result of a Solar Eclipse?

One of the earliest settlers along the Fraser River in Grand County was William Zane Cozens, fondly known as "Billy." He had been a law man in Gilpin County, but when he fell in love and married, he preempted and ranched the land which now forms the border between the towns of Winter Park and Fraser. The ranch house, which was a stage stop at the foot of Berthoud Pass on the route between Denver and Provo, Utah, was also the local post office. It has been preserved as a museum.

Tabernash was a Ute leader who could not accept the treaty of 1868 which laid out the Ute reservation to the west of Middle Park, one of the favorite hunting grounds of the Northern Utes. They had never been consulted on the "agreement," and did not have maps to show where Indian land and white territory divided. Tabernash was regarded with great apprehension by settlers who described him as a violent intruder with a vicious personality.

On July 29, 1878 there was a total eclipse of the sun. This was considered a foreboding of bad luck by some settlers who were not educated, but it was seen as an event of the century by others. To Tabernash, it seemed to be a divine sign which, after some meditation, he believed to be a signal to attack the newcomers to his beloved valley.

During the month of August farmers and ranchers were nervous, wondering what fate would bring. During that same time, Tabernash was rounding up a party of some forty Indians to attack the Cozens Ranch. As they gathered, Cozens sent a runner to Denver to request federal troops. Before the soldiers arrived, the Utes came down for the onslaught on September 1.

Billy Cozens met them with his rifle, but knowing the language quite well, he asked to talk to Tabernash. Before long the rancher had persuaded the Utes that some athletic contests to show off their skills would be welcome. Tabernash agreed, and the games began, continuing the entire day. Others at the ranch provided a feast of delicious refreshments. The Utes lost their inclination to massacre the whites.

By the time the troops arrived, the Indians had moved down the river and laid out a race track, enjoying their favorite sport of all—horse racing. A week later, they drifted back into the Gore Range to hunt. In another foray, Tabernash was shot and killed by a rancher. The town of Tabernash was named after him.

It was a year later when the Utes finally did have an uprising, killing all the men at the Northern Ute Agency of Nathan C. Meeker.

24

THE BEAVER CREEK MASSACRE

Wanton Slaughter of Ute Indians

While the infamous Sand Creek Massacre of Cheyenne Indians in 1864 stands as the greatest blot on the history of the white man in Colorado, another disgraceful attack on a small band of Utes has been all but forgotten, this in spite of the remark by Indian Agent C. T. Stollsteimer that, "It will always be a blot on the reputation of the country."

When the Southern Utes were banished to a reservation in the southwestern corner of Colorado in 1881, they were still permitted to hunt outside the boundary of their designated land. Probably true is that, in their bitterness, some may have found that a rancher's cow would do as well as a deer to bring home from the hunt. Several ranchers reported missing cattle to the United States militia at Fort Lewis near Durango.

That being the case, there was much resentment against the Utes among the newcomers. This was especially true in what was then known as the Big Bend area of the Dolores River, south of the town of Dolores. The region is now inundated by the McPhee Reservoir.

At daybreak on June 19, 1885 a gang of "white scoundrels" murdered a small group of Indians for no apparent reason. There were either six or eleven men, women and children in the band, depending on which account one chooses.

The slaughter occurred near the point where Beaver Creek flows into the Dolores River, and has been dubbed the Beaver Creek Massacre. None of the assailants were ever arrested, despite demands of the Indian agent.

As terrorism begets terrorism, which then leads to more terrorism, the incident threw the region into a state of panic. One rancher was apparently killed by Utes in retaliation, and some settlers fled their homes to hide in caves, fearing a full-fledged Ute uprising.

By July, thanks to the work of the capable Agent Stollsteimer, the fears diminished and affairs returned to normal. In justification, a county commissioner had written to a Dolores newspaper, "Every man (should) defend his person and property and . . . shoot every Indian that may be found in the country, no matter what his business may be."

This illustration shows the Utes crossing the Grand (Colorado) River to leave Colorado for what is now Utah in the fall of 1881. Courtesy of P. David Smith

25

AMERICANIZATION OF NATIVE AMERICANS

Grand Junction's Teller Institute

Lf you had been alive a century ago, you might have cheered the idea. Indians had been driven from their hunting grounds to live on reservations because Americans believed that God's will was that all men be Christians and do work based on agriculture. The aborigines must be allowed to learn proper work habits and discard their "pagan" religion to become strong, independent citizens.

Thus were founded two off-reservation schools in Western Colorado: Fort Lewis, a former military establishment at Hesperus, and the Teller Institute at Grand Junction, named for ex-Senator Henry Teller. Federal money was used to finance these schools where proper ideals of citizenship would be learned by native children of the Ute tribe.

Begun in 1886, the Teller Institute got off to a bad start, as only seven children were enrolled. The Northern Utes, now on the Uintah Reservation in Utah, were not at all enthused about their children being removed. (It is said that in Arizona, Navajo children were sometimes abducted forcibly in order to meet the quotas of such schools.)

The farmland which was donated to the school was about the worst in the Grand Valley; it was alkali-laden soil with very poor drainage. Efforts to grow fruits and vegetables there mostly met with failure.

By the time Teller Institute had grown to nearly 200 students, through massive recruitment from six other Native American tribes, the idea of "outings" was born. This meant that students would serve half a day in classes, and the rest of their hours would work on active

55

farms, "learning the art of agriculture." If there were payments for their labor, the money went to the school, not the student. Most of what the males learned was how to weed, dig ditches, and pick fruit. They were in demand during harvest season, being much, much cheaper than transient labor. The girls learned how to clean houses, wash dishes, and sew.

Students were given adequate instruction in English, manual training, and cooking. They were dressed in neat uniforms for public appearances, and had football teams, basketball teams, a band, mandolin orchestra and gave speeches on occasion.

While allowed to withdraw, they were not permitted to run away. In the early days, according to one eventual escapee named Turoose, the industrial teacher wore a loaded revolver. When Turoose and several other boys tried an earlier escape, they were chased by an armed "posse" of staff members and returned at gunpoint with threats of imprisonment or even hanging.

While it is not known whether any of the graduates of the eight years of instruction ever started a farm, it is possible that some may have had more opportunity for employment in menial jobs due to their knowledge of English. The girls could now earn a pittance as housekeepers and the boys knew how to dig ditches for irrigation. They may also have learned how to be obedient and to refrain from complaint in their jobs.

By 1911, it was decided that the program was not accomplishing what it was set up to do. Both the Fort Lewis school and the Teller Institute were abandoned for more practical purposes. Fort Lewis became an agricultural college which moved to Durango and later became a four-year state college. The Teller Institute was used by the state as a home for mental retardees; now known by the euphemism of "The Regional Center for Developmental Disabilities."

In the handy hindsight of history, the philanthropic ideals which founded the schools seem misguided, but then they were certainly well-intentioned.

26

MAKING SOUTHERN UTES INTO MODERN FARMERS

They Loved Their Chariots of Steel

In the waning years of the nineteenth century, officials of the United States Bureau of Indian Affairs became dismayed that many of their efforts to convert the Indians of the Southern Ute Reservation to farming had failed miserably. Some Utes still wanted to depend upon hunting and gathering, and they had always had a great infatuation for horse-racing. There were government stipends of food and clothing which made too many of the Indians dependent upon the government.

It was then that one of these Washington officials had a sudden realization. While their white neighbors were using modern horse-drawn machinery, the few Utes who did farm were still condemned to the back-breaking labors of spades, hoes and rakes.

Many thousands of dollars were used to supply the Utes with the most modern mowing machines and horse-drawn rakes. There was little instruction given as to the proper use of these technological miracles. In the words of pioneer observer Lena Knapp, "a staid farmer was supposed to be produced in a summer as a result of the experiment."

A few of the farming men on the reservation did learn on their own to use the machinery, but others were baffled until they found a better use. They removed the cutting bars from the mowing machines and some of the rake attachments. It was realized that they could then place the seats behind fast horses and scurry across the desert lands. Soon, these new-fangled chariots of steel were used for races, and the equipment furnished a new sport.

Some of the neighboring ranchers roamed the Ute lands and gathered the spare parts, which were strewn over the countryside, remaking them into workable entities.

The horse and horseracing was a very important part of the Ute culture. Courtesy of P. David Smith

Part Three

SPIRITUALISTS AND SAGES

There are interesting people everywhere, and they are the ones who most often create the incidents from which history draws its anecdotes. Some of these are brilliant, others are simply practical, some are vicious, others quite humorous. There are those who received messages from sources never revealed to others; there are those who simply go about their assigned tasks without being aware that they are, in retrospect, heroes or heroines. Included here are a few who lived in that lonely land west of the Great Divide.

27

SENSIBLE SETTLEMENT OF A UTE-NAVAJO WAR

Both Tribes Coveted Pagosa Springs

There had been much friction between the Navajos of the Southwest and the Utes of the mountains long before anyone of European background appeared.

The famous scout, Kit Carson, in his notorious and cruel round-up of Navajos during the Civil War, enlisted the help of Utes, allowing them to take any captured Navajo as a slave. The driving of the Navajo 200 miles to brutal prisons in eastern New Mexico might be classified as the southwest's own "Trail of Tears." Many died; the rest were driven from their ancestral homelands because the Union Army believed there was gold to be had in the desert. Carson's inhumane tactics are rarely mentioned in the glorified accounts of his career.

One of Carson's commanders in this atrocious campaign was Captain Albert Pfeiffer. Pfeiffer, who was born either in Holland or Scotland, depending on one's source, had been assigned to New Mexico in the 1850s. He married a Spanish woman, but had to be away for long periods of time. Apaches murdered his wife and her two servant girls on June 20, 1863, while they were bathing in one of New Mexico's hot springs. Somehow, the enraged Pfeiffer considered Apaches as being in league with Navajos, for whom he developed undying hatred.

Promoted to Lieutenant Colonel for his leadership in the rout of the Navajo, Pfeiffer was appointed Carson's assistant when the latter was made Commandant of Fort Garland, in the San Luis Valley. When Carson retired, Pfeiffer decided it was time for him to leave the military, and he settled on a ranch, where he became a good friend of the Utes. They adopted him into the tribe, designating him as Tata (Father) Pfeiffer.

In the early 1870s, both the Utes and the Navajos claimed the health-giving waters of Pagosa Springs. A war was waged between the tribes for several years and cost many lives. It was then that the leaders of the two factions held a truce and came up with one of the most sound solutions in history to end the conflict.

Rather than see hundreds more of their people die or become maimed, they decided to choose one man from each tribe and have a duel to the death, with the winning tribe having undisputed owner-ship of the springs. The Navajos chose a huge, powerful brave as their contestant. The Utes, however, had no sizable contender noted for his prowess in man-to-man combat. It was then that Col. Pfeiffer volunteered, providing he could choose the weapons.

Navajos agreed, providing that the fight be carried out totally in the nude, so that no concealed weapons could be carried. Pfeiffer selected the Bowie knife as the weapon. He'd had much experience using that weapon in combat.

On the appointed day, the two men, each naked as the day he was born, faced each other, holding the knives. After some maneu-vering in the enclosed arena, they faced each other with knives in the striking position. Pfeiffer stood two paces away from his enormous opponent, and, with a powerful thrust, threw his knife into the chest of the Navajo, who died within minutes.

True to their word, the Navajos withdrew for all time from the famous springs, and the Utes would have no more conflicts over their health spa until the white men expelled them to an adjoining reservation.

28

A TOOTHACHE LED TO A DISCOVERY

The Excruciating Pain of Mr. Marshall

It was in the fall of 1873. One branch of the noted Wheeler Survey had been exploring the San Juan Mountains at a site near what is now the town of Silverton. Winter seemed to be setting in a bit early, so the party, under the command of William Marshall, decided to return to Denver.

(As it turned out, that winter was exceptionally bad, being the one which marooned the Alferd Packer party in another section of those mountains. It resulted in Packer killing and devouring his comrades in order to survive.)

The route was to take the surveyors through the San Luis Valley, but early in the travel, Marshall developed a severe toothache. It was so bad, and his jaw was so swollen, that he had to sip gruel through a straw. He later described it as "one of the worst toothaches that ever befell a mortal." The long journey would take nearly a month. The victim considered having the blacksmith extract the molar, but instead decided to try for a shortcut to Denver.

With him was a packer, David Mears. After finally getting out of the arduous San Juans, they were faced with the formidable Sawatch Range, highest in the state. By that time the snow was becoming so deep that crossing any pass of over 11,000 feet would be impossible, but Marshall recalled seeing a dip between what would later be named Mount Ouray and Windy Peak. This location is about ten miles south of the modern Monarch Pass, between Salida and Gunnison.

They decided to try this notch. It took six days, struggling over fallen timber and through the snows, to reach the summit of 10,600 feet. Once there, Marshall almost forgot his pain in the excitement of finding a pass with a fairly gradual grade on both sides; it would even be possible for a railroad to cross at that level.

When the two men reached Denver, they figured they had cut 125 miles from the route. The rest of the entourage reached town four days later. Marshall had by that time been to the dentist, and spread the word of the discovery in Denver. A few years later, Marshall Pass, as it became known, was a key transportation route to the Western Slope, and eventually the route of the Denver and Rio Grande Railway.

Marshall Pass was a critical link for trains passing east and west at the turn of the century. Courtesy of P. David Smith

29

JITTERY DAYS FOLLOWING THE UTE UPRISING

How to Get a Free Beer

In September of 1879 the Northern Ute Indians had "had it" with Agent Nathan C. Meeker. They revolted and killed the agency men, as well as ambushing an army unit coming to the rescue. This carnage caused much apprehension throughout the mining towns which had been permitted to exist on the Ute Reservation.

It was a cold October evening when a man by the name of McCann came running into a saloon in Howardsville, a mining town northeast of Silverton. He had jumped from his horse and screamed to the men at the bar, "Git up and git out of here! The Indians have massacred everybody in Animas City and are moving toward Silverton. I have dispatches for the governor for arms and troops and am going to Antelope Springs before daylight. Bartender, give me a drink!"

McCann got his beer. He had invented the entire drama because he was very thirsty and very much out of pocket. He confessed, and the crowd calmed down, buying him several other rounds.

30

SPIRITUALIST MINER OF THE MASTER KEY

Only Dead Wives Could Tell Where the Gold Was

Tom Kleckner arrived in the Hahn's Peak region of Routt County in 1895. At the age of forty, he had apparently found himself a failure, and after the financial panic of 1893, he decided to look for gold. In the ensuing years he had some minor successes with mines named the Hidden Treasure, Little Joe, Prospector and Ohio Boy. These mines gave forth a little silver and other minerals, but no gold to speak of.

There seems to be some confusion about whether he was married at that time. If so, it was to one of two wives whom he called "Ella." There was a great wave of interest in spiritualism during the first two decades of the twentieth century. Somehow, Tom was drawn to the practice, combining it with socialism he had acquired during his struggles.

A person who knew him before 1920 swore that he would sit around the grave of his dear, departed Ella and have visits with her. He would place sticks around the burial site, and observe them moving into different positions. As a result of these seances, presumably, he founded the Master Key Mine.

He had visions of making a great discovery of gold which would bring 50,000 people to the spot north of Columbine, where his ownership was identified (with the weird name and punctuation) as "The Kleckner Mutual COOPERATIVE Society of the W O R L D."

He was later to have a wife who was also known as Ella. Now in his sixties, he on one occasion directed miners working for him to disregard what appeared to be a good vein of silver, and dig in a different direction for a spot where he felt there was gold.

By the time of the Great Depression of the 1930s, Tom became desperate for money, and had to let his employees go. Finally, in 1935 at the age of eighty, he took a butcher knife and chased Ella with it. He realized that alive she could not tell him where the gold was, dead she could give him the answer. Ella ran terrified to some neighbors. They put her on the stage back to her Ohio home. She never returned.

His last fleeting hope for a revelation gone, Kleckner pined away and died the next year. He had failed to establish his socialist dream, to gain wealth, or to get the "master key" from beyond the grave of his wife, or wives.

These men, like thousands of others, came to Colorado in search of gold. Courtesy of P. David Smith Marvels of the New West, *1887*

31

A SOUTHWEST "NORTHWEST PASSAGE"

Sam Adams' Dream Ended in Gore Canyon

For hundreds of years Europeans had looked for a "Northwest Passage" which would enable ships to go from the Atlantic to the Pacific Oceans. It was never realized, although a nuclear submarine has made it under the Arctic icecap. At one time the United States Government offered a prize of $3,750 or more for anyone who would find such a route.

It was years before the time that a crackpot was able to convince a Denver newspaper that he could dredge the Platte River through Nebraska and the South Platte to Denver, thus opening Denver to Transatlantic shipping.

The mining town of Breckenridge, on the Blue River, had gone into a slump when placer mining gave out in 1869. The most important man in that community was Judge Marshall Silverthorne, after whom a town would be named beneath the Dillon Dam a century later. Things were rather gloomy in Breckenridge, with many unemployed miners.

It was then that an adventurer named "Captain" Samuel Adams showed up and convinced Silverthorne and several other civic leaders that there was truly a "Northwest Passage" and that the Federal Government still had the bounty listed.

Boats could be built and go down the Blue to its confluence with the Colorado River, and thence through the Grand Canyon to the Gulf of Lower California! As word got around illimitable excitement swept the town.

Citizens jumped to volunteer, building four wooden boats out of green pine, and eagerly applying to Captain Adams to be appointed to his crew of ten men who would make the premier voyage. Both the boat builders and crew would share in the reward money, as well as anyone furnishing supplies for the venture. Ladies made a huge banner for the send-off which read "Western Colorado to California - Greetings!"

When all was ready, the town turned out to hear Marshall Silverthorne give a speech extolling the historic significance of the moment. He presented Adams with a dog to accompany the party, and a goodly supply of his wife's homemade bread.

Thus, the "Breckenridge Navy" was launched.

Somehow all four boats made it to the Colorado River (then called the Grand River), although many of the "sailors" were beginning to have doubts that their crafts were able to sustain some of the whitewater rapids. A few "jumped ship" at the overnight stop on the banks of the Colorado. By the time the four boats reached the lower Gore Canyon, they were swept against rocks and damaged, some sinking immediately. Fortunately, all crew members and the dog survived as the expedition came to an end, and no reward was given for the valiant effort.

32

GARWOOD JUDD: "THE MAN WHO STAYED"
A Gothic Tale

July and August are delightful months to visit the Crested Butte region. It has been proclaimed "Colorado's Wildflower Capitol" by the governor.

About ten miles above Crested Butte, the ghost town of Gothic is nestled in an exceptionally lush meadowland tucked among towering peaks. It is currently the home of the Rocky Mountain Biological Laboratory. Several nationally famous biologists make their summer homes there. Scholars converge on the old mining camp to observe the diverse plant growth and to philosophize.

Gothic had only one resident remaining in 1928, when Western State College biologist John C. Johnson purchased the townsite for only $200 in overdue taxes and established the laboratory. That denizen was Garwood Hall Judd, who has ever since been remembered as "the man who stayed." Judd died only two years later, but his memory has been preserved in the name of an exquisite waterfall about a half mile above the town on the Copper Creek trail. There, a stone bench has been built, on which one may meditate in view of one of the state's truly charming vistas.

Who was this man, Judd? He arrived there in 1879, in the boom days of Gothic. The Sylvanite Mine at the head of Copper Creek produced rich deposits of wire silver. The mine continued its cornucopia of riches for the next six years. However, from that time on, fewer and fewer pockets of the precious wire were found, and by 1914 the post office had closed forever.

Garwood, who was only twenty-seven years old when he arrived, soon became discouraged with prospecting, and opted for the more dependable vocation as a saloonkeeper. Eventually he became the perennial mayor of Gothic. It was he who was first to welcome former President Ulysses S. Grant, who, on an 1880 tour of the West, went there to visit a "real, wild, mining camp in action."

Judd apparently never married. There was a story told that he had been betrothed to a lovely woman who succumbed to smallpox a month before their wedding date. As the fortunes of Gothic dwindled, he was at last alone there.

The late Dr. Lois Borland, venerable English professor at Gunnison's Western State College, wrote about him in an unpublished narrative found after her passing. She referred to him as "one of her friends in high places." (Gothic's elevation is nearly 9,500 feet above sea level.) She visited him from time to time in the 1920s.

Miss Borland wrote, "He stood outside the door to welcome us, sinewy and slender, shrewd and bantering—a Yankee monarch of the beauty and desolation surrounding him. His seventy-odd years do not obtrude, even though people call him Old Mister Judd. Only once, when he came to town below to recuperate after a long sickness alone in the hills, I remember he was yellow and slightly bowed, and that his wonted banter was forced."

She believed this hermit to be well-educated, according to his manner of speech. Borland noted that he used a typewriter which was kept in the back room to write letters, hoping to attract Eastern capital to re-open the mines of Gothic.

Gothic Mountain looms above the village with its almost vertical face. The peak sends down so many snowslides that this site has been a haven for winter study by avalanche experts in more recent years. While rarely hitting the town, they thunder down over the roads and paths on either side of Gothic. Judd never did let one catch him as he slid down to Crested Butte on skis to stock up on supplies.

No one seems to be sure how he obtained the money for his scant needs. He did receive a modest stipend in 1928, when Hollywood's Fox Film Company went to the ghost town to make a two-reel movie about the recluse, who still called himself mayor.

After he died at the age of seventy-eight, his ashes were scattered over his beloved, deserted "city." Today, his waterfall still flows and hikers still pause to repose on "Judd's Bench."

33

PAT DAWSON'S TERRIBLE COFFEE

"Bitter as Bile and Black as Coal"

Being a chuckwagon cook on roundups was a very demanding job. The cook would usually rise at 3:30 A.M. and start a pot of coffee boiling. He was usually busy about eighteen hours a day, week after week. For this reason, many cooks were considered rather ill-tempered, as is also said of many restaurant chefs.

Pat Dawson was a good cook on an outfit up in northern Routt County, but he had a short fuse. It was the job of the nighthawk, the cowboy assigned to watch over the horses at night, to bring in wood for the morning fire, and in most cases, start the fire. There were different woods preferred for various purposes. Scrub oak was the longest-burning; sagebrush knots made the hottest fires for baking.

Pat was a pipe smoker. When he wasn't puffing away or clenching the dead pipe in his teeth, he would slip it into his shirt pocket. No one ever saw him clean the pipe.

One morning, when a new man assigned as nighthawk brought in the wrong wood for fuel, Pat ran him off with a club, and then lit his pipe to relax and make the most of the situation. Occasionally his biscuits had little specks in them, which the boys knew were ashes from his pipe. On the whole they liked his meals and were cowed by his authoritarian ways.

One exception was his terrible coffee. He would simply put some newly-ground coffee on top of the previous day's grounds in the five-gallon pail, and let it simmer. According to John Rolfe Burroughs, who related this story in his book, *Where the Old West*

71

Stayed Young, the resulting brew was "bitter as bile and black as coal." Nevertheless, the hands did not dare complain.

Then came the day when Pat found that his pipe was missing. They were at least fifty miles away from any place where a substitute could be found. Dawson went into a deep funk, and accused the men of stealing the pipe. As the days went on, the coffee became worse, with several days of old grounds in it.

Another new cowhand, who was not yet acquainted with the cook's formidable temperament, rebelled. Swearing he would no longer "strangle on that poison," he committed the revolutionary act of kicking the pail over, spilling all the coffee.

It was then discovered that under the grounds was Pat's pipe, which must have fallen out of his pocket a week earlier, and had been subject to its first real cleaning. Pat dried it off, lit it up, and thanked the recruit for rescuing his beloved friend.

It was reported that while Pat was a bit more agreeable, his coffee never improved noticeably.

34

THE NIMBLE FINGERS OF
THE LAY POSTMASTER

Wallihan's Pioneer Wildlife Shots

In Moffat County there is hardly anything left of what was the town of Lay. In the 1870s it served as a federal supply camp for the Northern Ute Indians. After the territory was opened to settlement by ranchers, Lay was still a trading village in the bleak rangeland.

After coming from Wisconsin to Denver and then Leadville, A. G. Wallihan went to Lay as postmaster. His wife, identified only in records as Mrs. Wallihan, was his companion in that isolated country.

A destitute itinerant missionary stopped by and was given food and shelter by the Wallihans. He showed them a camera he had no need to keep, so Mrs. Wallihan bought it from him. Together, the Wallihans learned how to load the camera with dry plates. Then studying books, they mastered the techniques of darkroom developing.

By 1888, the pair was able to go out and become so familiar with the wildlife that deer would come close enough to be photographed. Then they were more confident, and in one case, took a picture of a cougar leaping from a tree. Wallihan had learned perfect timing and could snap the shutter quickly on the old camera.

His photographs soon attracted national attention. They were among the first such nature studies. In 1894, the Wallihans published a book, *Hoofs, Claws and Antlers of the Rocky Mountains.* The introduction was written by Theodore Roosevelt. Reissued in 1902, it bore an introduction by William F. "Buffalo Bill" Cody. A later even more exciting book, *Camera Shots at Big Game,* carried the endorsement of Roosevelt once more, this time as President of the United States.

At that time, the most famous naturalist in the nation was William T. Horaday. He noted that Americans owed a greater debt to Wallihan than to any other man of his time. Horaday failed to note that the books always listed as author-photographers, "Mr. and *Mrs.* A.G. Wallihan."

The couple kept pace with more sophisticated equipment when developed, and their quick reactions in the field became models for later nature photographers.

Wallihan died in 1935. He had found time to sculpt beautiful caskets for himself and his wife. Mrs. Wallihan followed him shortly afterward.

This is Wallihan's famous 1895 photograph of a cougar jumping out of a tree. Courtesy of Colorado Historical Society Rocky Mountain Photo Co.

35

MR. OSGOOD'S AMAZING OLDSMOBILE

. . .And Teddy Roosevelt's Easiest Game Hunt

At the beginning of the twentieth century, John Cleveland Osgood was the owner of the Colorado Fuel and Iron Company, which was the biggest steel producer west of the Mississippi. At Redstone, the model coal mining town he created, he built the luxurious Cleveholm Manor (now popularly called "Redstone Castle") on his 4,200 acre estate.

Cleveholm was host to many prominent businessmen and political leaders of the time. Osgood was the first person in those parts to own an automobile. It was a sleek little 1901 Oldsmobile two-seater. On one occasion, he treated each of the visitors to a ride in his car.

It was then that he boasted that his Olds could climb the precarious zig-zag trail that led up from the Redstone area to McClure Pass, almost a half mile higher than the Crystal River canyon in which Cleveholm stood. His guests challenged him, saying they couldn't ever imagine the day when any motor car could make it up to that pass.

The next morning the guests were invited on a hunting trip up the hazardous trail. When they arrived at the summit, there reflecting the sunlight was the little Oldsmobile! The hunters were stunned!

It is part of the lore that no one ever got around to telling them that Osgood had put his men at Cleveholm to work all night, dismantling the car and packing it up by light of lanterns to the top of McClure, and then reassembling the remarkable automobile before dawn.

Another visitor at Cleveholm was President Theodore Roosevelt on one of his famous big game hunting forays into Western Colorado. The hunt had not netted much on that autumn day. The two men sat down in rocking chairs on the capacious veranda fronting the mansion to watch the evening shadows gather. For some reason, Roosevelt had his rifle beside him.

Soon a deer scurried across the spacious lawn before them, quickly followed by an elk with a massive rack. It is said that there were dozens of game animals for the President to shoot from his comfortable position. He apparently downed two of the animals before he realized that Osgood had arranged for the resident gamekeeper to herd them across the greens.

Redstone Castle was built about 1903 by J. C. Osgood at a cost of $500,000. Author's collection

36

THE SECRET TRAVELS OF A MONARCH?

Cruel Despot of the Congo

The stories are all over the mountains. King Leopold II, of Belgium, was the only crowned head ever to cross the Colorado Divide to visit the Western Slope. He swam in the Glenwood Hot Springs pool; he stayed at the Jerome Hotel in Aspen; he was a guest of John C. Osgood at Cleveholm, the so-called Redstone Castle.

Most dramatic of all is the account of how he was demonstrating his mountain-climbing ability on the balconies of Ouray's Beaumont Hotel when he fell and landed safely on a couch. That's quite a trick for a man who would have had to be over sixty-eight years old at the time. Furthermore, as Ouray historians P. David Smith and Marvin Gregory have noted, the story of his visit to Ouray never was printed until the 1950s.

His other visits seem to have been kept secret, too. The only one which has some possible supporting evidence is as a guest at Cleveholm Manor in Redstone. Since Cleveholm was built in 1903, and Leopold was born in 1835, the king would have been quite old at that time. He died in 1909, age 74, one of the most detested men in the world.

A global traveler and noted athlete, Leopold was also the owner of the Congo as personal property after its conquest by Belgium. Taking a special interest in the crown colony, the king enslaved the entire black population and reaped millions of dollars for himself.

He was a believer in white superiority and became noted for his cruelties to blacks. They were kept in a state of abject poverty and literally driven by the whip. Gradually the world became aware of

Leopold's sadistic practice of having the hands cut off men, women and children whom he considered less than obedient.

It is true that he promoted some development in Africa, sending the famous Dr. Livingston as a missionary physician to the interior. Years later the *New York Herald* sent Henry Stanley to find the missing man of the cloth. However, Leopold became a subject of disgust throughout the civilized world for his inhumane exploitation. Finally in 1908, the colony was relinquished to the ownership of Belgium, although the natives were not treated much better.

Even the 1911 *Encyclopedia Britannica*, noted for its objectivity and detail, recorded that Leopold's reputation had been destroyed years before that time. It was in those years, if he really came to Western Colorado, that he probably traveled secretly with his entourage.

37

THE WEST'S MOST EXTRAORDINARY HERMIT

Pat Lynch of Pat's Hole

Echo Park is located where the Yampa River flows into the Green River. It is now a part of Dinosaur National Monument in Moffat County. The spot was so named by John Wesley Powell in his famous 1869 expedition down the tributaries of the Colorado River and through the Grand Canyon. At that point, there is a monolith now known as Echo Rock, but also called Steamboat Rock, towering some 800 feet over the confluence of the rivers. It has been said that sentences of ten words or more can be reflected, sometimes more than once, from the prominence.

Echo Park is often referred to as "Pat's Hole" because of a man who lived there for many years, first in a cave, and later in a small cabin. That man was Pat Lynch who found his way to the secluded spot after an already colorful life.

Pat told many stories, and they may have been true; at least they were consistent in the memories of the ranchers who knew him. A native of Ireland, he had served on a sailing vessel when he was fourteen years of age. Shipwrecked on the coast of Africa, he was captured by natives and spent several years rising to a position of prominence in a tribe. He was later rescued and taken to India on an English ship.

Migrating to America at the beginning of the Civil War, Pat enlisted in the Union Navy. According to his account, he threw off a bomb which had landed on the deck of his ship but was injured in the process, so he was discharged from that service. He did however qualify for the army and took part in the Plains Indian wars. After that he went to Denver and then to western Colorado where he lived in outdoor natural surroundings.

Finally establishing himself at Echo Park, Lynch became a legend partly because of his relationship to the wild animals there. He would not kill an animal but would make jerky out of the flesh of already dead creatures. He had pet beaver and deer. He was most proud, however, of a mountain lion which would bring him deer meat. The lion hung out some distance from the cabin, and whenever Pat called it, the lion would answer back. Because the sound was so lovely to Pat, he called the feline Jenny Lind, after a famous singer of the time. Thus a nearby formation is known as Jenny Lind Rock, former habitat of the lion.

It was also said that he tamed a wild horse, and would ride the animal the ten miles to the nearest ranch to pick up his military pension. Pat subscribed to several newspapers and magazines, including the *Literary Digest*.

In all, he spent nineteen years in that lonely spot. Pat Lynch died in 1917 at the reported age of nearly ninety-nine. One writer called him the West's most extraordinary hermit.

38

PULLEYS AND WEIGHTS FOR BROKEN HIPS

How a Durango Surgeon Gained International Fame

In the late 1870s, thirty-year-old Dr. W.R. Winters left his practice at the Port of New York and set up an office in the town of Parrot City in the San Juan Mountains. When the mining boom ended there, he moved to Durango where he gained respect as a very talented surgeon.

When there was a critical emergency, the railroad would speed him by special train to the site. On two occasions he was able to save the lives and preserve the mental capacity of people whose axe heads had flown off and split their skulls.

A problem which perplexed him was that of broken hips. Apparently no one had ever been able to prevent a crooked and hence shortened leg after a break in the hip. Winters pondered various methods by which the hip might be set in its original form to allow the patient to walk normally.

In 1889 a young miner in Silverton broke his hip when hit by a falling rock. Dr. Winters arrived there, and after examining the patient, went to the local hardware store and purchased pulleys, weights, rope and other equipment. He recruited a carpenter to construct a wooden framework above the patient's bed.

With a tackle he tightened the leg and held the break in place. This set the hip in proper formation, and as the doctor had hoped, the edges knit properly and the miner had a straight leg.

Winters was very pleased with the success and wrote a detailed article, complete with diagrams of the rigging. It was published in the *Journal of the American Medical Association*, and he received considerable acclaim. Never did he consider patenting the device, and it was available to the profession world-wide.

In 1896 Dr. Winters betook himself of a tour of Europe. Visiting a large London hospital he was surprised at the welcome he received, his invention being in wide use there. The staff provided him with introductions in Paris, Vienna, and Berlin, where he was accorded many courtesies.

He eventually removed his practice to Silverton, but he became ill and could no longer perform his medical work. Alone and somewhat poverty stricken, Dr. Winters died in the All Nations Boarding House in 1903. He was buried in the Hillside Cemetery of that town.

This rough camp in the Flat Tops area is typical of the one used by Carhart, Rainey and McFadden. Courtesy of Museum of Western Colorado Research Center and Special Library.

39

LEAVING THE WILDERNESS WILD

Three Happy Campers at Trappers Lake

When the Department of the Interior turned the National Forests over to the Department of Agriculture in 1905, the idea seemed logical. Trees and grazing were the main concerns, and they were both forms of agriculture. Interior still controlled National Parks and Monuments, places designed for recreational use.

It was about twelve years later that foresters began to notice an increase in visitors to the National Forests who sought recreation. Many of them hunted and fished in the White River National Forest among the "Flat Tops" north of Glenwood Springs. Officials had been liberal in giving out leases for cabins in all National Forests with little regard to preservation of the wilderness. With a realization that primitive areas were disappearing, they established a position known as "recreational engineer" to allot sites for roads and cabins.

One of the first men to fill this position was Arthur Hawthorne Carhart. He had graduated with a degree in landscape architecture from Iowa State College in 1917, just as the United States was drawn into World War I. Carhart served in the army and upon release in 1919, joined the Forest Service which assigned him to its Denver district office.

In response to considerable demand, the Denver office assigned Carhart to plot several hundred homesites and a road encircling the lovely Trappers Lake nestled beneath the Flat Tops formations. He set up his tent near the cabin of Scott Teague at the outlet of the lake. Teague had invited two men, Paul Rainey and William McFadden, as his guests that July in 1919.

Paul Rainey was a famous wildlife photographer who had brought the first motion pictures of African animal life to the United States. William McFadden was a successful financier who was instrumental in the development of oil drilling in Oklahoma. The two were enjoying a fishing vacation.

Carhart proceeded to make his surveys, and at the end of the day he joined Rainey and McFadden by a campfire as they watched the evening shadows gather around the pristine lake. After what Carhart later described as "spirited discussions," all three agreed that the resplendent beauty of the scene would be badly disturbed if the area was developed as planned. This conversation triggered the imaginative mind of the forester, and he conceived the idea that certain areas should be preserved as wilderness with no roads and no cabins at all.

Returning to Denver Carhart turned in the assigned survey to his superior, Carl J. Stahl. The report had at the end "an unsolicited comment" which Stahl found to be most interesting—the idea of doing nothing at all to the area! Stahl called attention to other foresters regarding Carhart's idea. When Aldo Leopold, an Albuquerque ranger, read the report, he led a personal campaign endorsing the concept of primitive reserves in National Forests. Carhart was then sent to Superior National Forest in Minnesota to plan a similar wilderness region. These two "de facto" experiments were maintained against considerable opposition during the decade of the twenties. Thus was born the Flat Tops Wilderness Area of White River National Forest.

By 1928 both were made official and gradually many other forests established wilderness areas. By 1964 the officials in Washington promoted the idea for all of the National Forests.

Against much opposition, the Bureau of Land Management has also begun to designate "wilderness study areas" free of roads and structures.

While most sources credit Leopold with the idea, he himself credited Carhart. Carhart, in turn, pointed out that it was simply an idea that developed when three happy campers were having a discussion at Trappers Lake.

40

"SAGE OF THE SAGEBRUSH"

Dan Hunter and the Dove Creek Press

Native Texan Dan Hunter had lived many lives before he arrived at Dove Creek, ten miles from the Utah border, in 1918. A graduate of Southwestern University in Georgetown, Texas, he had spent time in Mexico in copper mining and was a member of a Smithsonian expedition to the Mayan ruins in the Yucatan. Later he ran a grocery in his home state, became an oil executive, managed a large ranch and helped form the first mass transportation system in Dallas.

After all of that he yearned for a 320 acre homestead in the newly-developed sagebrush country at Dove Creek. He and his wife began farming and boosting the virtues of that remote land a hundred miles from any railroad. They were instrumental in forming the first school district there, and he taught all the subjects in the high school. Next he and his wife, Loula, built a hotel and restaurant.

Dan served in many civic roles and was active in the establishment of the first rural electrification of the region. By 1940, when Dove Creek had grown to a community of 400 population, Hunter was sixty-six years old but ready to try a new enterprise. Without any previous printing experience he founded the *Dove Creek Press,* a hand-set weekly publication. With his great vocabulary power, he established a literary style which has been regarded as unique in the annals of western journalism.

In such a small isolated place, the death of a citizen was major news, and Hunter became a master at writing obituaries. His elaborate imagination made masterpieces of what is usually a dull, routine function in journalism. For example, "We all shiver under the cold touch of death, but why grieve for her, for now she rests on a golden throne and forgets to weep. Tremulous hands of angels loosed for her the strings of life and she died."

Another sampling: "He has shrunken into the casket of death, which has been sealed with a seal of doom and has been cast down deep into the rolling tides of time: he has entered into the sacred bridal-gloom of death where he holds his nuptials with eternity. For each of us life is a grand tragedy, but over the ruins a glory shines. Then it is that 'We long for the touch of a vanished hand and the sound of a voice that is still.' "

Some editors agreed that he was "the most descriptive writer of his time," while others called his obituaries "profound nonsense." *New Yorker* magazine would quote him in sarcastic jest perhaps. One account stated that Colonel Robert R. McCormick made a trip to Dove Creek to ask about his willingness to write for the *Chicago Tribune*.

Historian Al Look included these criticisms and many others in his book, *Unforgettable Characters of Western Colorado*. Hunter sold his newspaper in 1945, and then spent another dozen years devoted to travel and promotion of Dove Creek. He died there in 1958.

It was Look who labeled Hunter the "Sage of the Sagebrush." Among other eloquent writings of Hunter were:

"Beyond the purple rim of dying day in the golden bars of Eventide."

"Our heart was crushed and our lips were dumb."

"In a quiet tomb where fond thoughts and gentle memories linger near, God hides some souls away sweetly to surprise us on judgment day."

"Seventy-one years of time has ploughed my cheek."

"Winter may continue until it chills the lap of May."

"I had rather anger a king than bring fear to the face of a child."

"The heavens bended low over our heads."

"The art of life is the process of selection."

"Tractors smashing the mud like bygone dinosaurs at play."

"Hope blinds me to the past and links me to the future."

41

THE WANDERING JEW OF THE RIO BLANCO COUNTRY

Eugene Voeltzel's Philosophic Ads

There is still a store at Rio Blanco, where the Piceance Creek Road joins State Highway 13, between Meeker and Rifle. During the 1930s, the store was owned by Eugene Voeltzel and his second wife, Pearl. Eugene always called himself "the Jew." His wife was a loyal member of the Meeker Rebekah Lodge.

Voeltzel was born in Strasburg, France, in 1878. His family had been victimized and stripped of all their property by the anti-Semitic Kaiser following the German victory in the Franco-Prussian War. They migrated to the United States, and Eugene grew up in Kansas City. He worked up from section hand to engineer on the Santa Fe Railroad, but fell victim to the great flu epidemic following World War I. He came to Colorado to recuperate. A married man, he started a store at Axial, a village south of Craig.

When the store burned down in 1929, all his investments except for a few horses were lost. In order to protect himself in bankruptcy, Gene signed over his possessions to his wife, and two or three weeks later she divorced him.

In 1930 he married Pearl Jones Vinson and started over with a store in Meeker, but failing in that, he turned to the art of cooking for sheepherders. The recipients of his culinary skill declared that he served up the best food that they had ever eaten. According to Voeltzel himself, the sheepherders commented, "That damn Jew made everything but waffles. He even tried that. He flattened them on the ground and ran the sheep over them to punch the holes, and the sheep jumped them and wouldn't make no holes!"

Pearl was a Methodist and wanted to get back to the region of her church, so the couple bought the Rio Blanco store. Voeltzel would run advertisements in the Meeker Herald for his enterprise which became keepsakes. For instance:

NEW DISCOVERY
An article in the *Denver Post* says a
Japanese scientist finds an old Chinese
formula of ground moose horns which grows
hair on bald heads and is a sex restorative.
We have made application for some of the powders.
Stop for Gas at Rifle Price and Cold Drinks.
We might have the powders.
The Jew

and:
American women have come into their own.
Paris styles say they must have hips and busts.
Lots more rest for our millions of men, PWA
says. (New Deal Public Works Administration)
Buy foreign steel because it is 15% cheaper.
Please approach Piceance and Rio Blanco
intersection carefully for baby carriages have
the right-of-way over autos and mine might be
crossing!
The Jew

After moving back to Meeker where they engaged in many other ventures, Pearl died in 1967. Gene followed her in 1970. He was remembered throughout both Moffat and Rio Blanco Counties, and his ads are still on display at the White River Museum in Meeker.

42

COUNTING SHEEP FOR SIXTY-FIVE YEARS

Tony Garcia: the Quintessential Shepherd

He traced his heritage back to Diego Vargas, a member of the Cortez conquest of Mexico. Tony Epifanio Garcia may have been the most dedicated sheepherder in Colorado, if not the West, with a continuous career of sixty five years.

Born in 1905 at Ojo Caliente, New Mexico, Tony was only fourteen years of age when he had to quit school to take over the flock his father tended. At that time the family was living in Hot Springs (now known as Truth or Consequences), when Tony's dad went blind and could no longer continue as a sheepherder.

From that time on, the youth grew to be an expert in the responsibilities which demanded fifteen hours a day most of the year around.

It was this life he continued until the age of seventy-nine, and even after that he took some shorter stints in the field.

In 1934 when he was twenty-nine years old, Tony married Genevieve, and they had seven children. The family would often visit him in his trailer where he watched over thousands of sheep. In 1949 the family moved to the town of Hotchkiss where they felt their children could get a better education than in New Mexico. In that region, the North Fork of the Gunnison River, Tony worked for almost every sheep rancher.

His day usually began at 3:30 in the morning, when he would prepare a good breakfast and then feed his dogs and two horses. Over the years he had many well-trained dogs, mostly Australian blue collies. The work day normally ended late in the afternoon when it was time to fix supper and get some sleep.

Tony knew about all there was to know about raising sheep. He was called upon many times by other sheepmen to help at difficult births, wherein he could turn the lamb around when only one leg was out and give it a normal delivery.

He would usually move the flocks every ten days so that there would be no overgrazing. When the blizzards came up, he would have to stop the sheep who would often stampede. If they hit a fence they might smother each other in the panic.

Another threat was that of attacks by coyotes, mountain lions or bears. On one occasion Garcia was cutting through some bushes when his horse signaled danger. Tony looked up to see an eight foot brown bear charging at him. He took a quick and accurate shot with his rifle, killing the predator, but Tony reported that he had the shakes when he tried to get back on his horse.

In 1965 the sheepherder was camped up near Electric Mountain, north of Paonia. It was a cold day, and the early snow was very deep. Suddenly he felt an intense pain and realized that he was having an attack of appendicitis. He was more than four miles from any ranch house. The appendix had apparently nearly burst as he tried to stagger for help, but kept falling down in agony. Every time he fell, his faithful dog would lick his face to revive him. When Tony finally got to the ranch, a doctor was summoned. The medic claimed that the snow he had fallen on had actually frozen the appendix and thus saved his life. Garcia could never forget his gratitude to that devoted dog.

A few years later, Tony was bucked off his horse and the horse fell on him, breaking several of his ribs. He finally climbed back on the mount and rode to his trailer, sending his horse to find help. When a rancher saw a horse without a rider, he knew someone was in trouble. The herder was rescued but had to spend a long time in the hospital, suffering excruciating pain. Later in his career, he was fated to break those ribs again.

Garcia was a very religious man. He kept both a Spanish and English Bible with him and read them regularly. His son, Tony, said that his father always had his paychecks sent to the Hotchkiss home, where the family was well taken care of by Genevieve who was four years younger than her husband.

At last the old sheepherder decided that a full-time job was getting to be a little too much, so he dropped his lifetime routine at the age of seventy-nine, undertaking a new challenge. He learned to drive a car, although his son reported that it was always a bit complicated for him. He even drove with the heater going in the summer.

Tony Garcia died in 1992 at the age of eighty-seven. He was among the very last of the old style career sheepherders in the West.

Even today travelers are often stopped in the Colorado mountains to wait for a sheep herd to pass. Author's Collection

43

COLORADO'S TOUGHEST GAME WARDEN

He Had Been Jailed for Poaching

In 1903 there were so few deer left in West Central Colorado that all big game hunting had been banned, and it was an event that drew crowds when a deer was sighted. There were almost no elk left as ranchers and miners had supplemented their diets liberally with the tasty wapiti. The Aspen Elks Lodge had some elk imported from Wyoming, and those were presumably the forerunners of many thousands which roam the region today.

Bill Kreutzer, the nation's first forest service ranger, was stationed at Cedaredge at that time. A lady of that town was officially designated as game warden, but she didn't get out often, and so appointed Kreutzer as her field representative. That was when he discovered five elk carcasses hanging in a shed owned by Ott Peterson. Peterson had previous troubles with Kreutzer over illegal cutting of timber on Grand Mesa.

It was a real problem for Kreutzer to get a warrant for the arrest of Peterson, as the local judge did not want to rock the boat with legal action, but Kreutzer threatened to spread the word of illegal poaching if the warrant was not signed, thus sending Peterson to the Delta County Jail for several weeks.

A decade passed during which Kreutzer was promoted to Chief Ranger of the Gunnison National Forest, stationed in Gunnison. One day, in walked Ott Peterson sporting a badge of the State of Colorado. He had become a game warden, he said, because he had respected the tenacity of Kreutzer in that case so long ago.

Peterson was described as the most hated and feared warden in the state. He would relentlessly pursue suspects, even getting injured in a shoot-out on Black Mesa near Crawford, at one time. While he was the nemesis of many poachers, most accounts of his career praise him as a man who was totally dedicated to law and order.

Ott may have been tough, but he was fair. The official history of the Colorado Wildlife Service has a special section devoted to his career; his integrity as well as his dedication have become something of a model.

He dropped his discipline on only one occasion, and that event has spawned various stories. Rancher Clint Roeber remembers that when the elk herd had grown, a rancher called on Ott to shoot one which had been bothering the stock. After he had killed the elk and was hauling it in a wagon, a barefoot boy who did not know this scourge of the poachers came up and said it looked as though Ott had his winter's meat supply. The child added, "I don't blame you. We got one hanging up in our cabin, too."

Peterson later recalled that he went into the cabin and found the venison. After looking over the home of the impoverished family and realizing that none of the children had shoes, he said in his words, "There was nothin' else for those kids to eat. I just turned around and walked off. That was the only feller I ever let go. I just couldn't arrest him."

According to another rancher, Ott would go into the home of any suspect and rip the covers off beds, and open crocks of mincemeat, apparently flashing his search warrant.

He and Kreutzer had become good friends and worked together on some investigations involving forest lands. Peterson was said to have made arrests in all sixty-three counties of Colorado. Ott's career ended only with his death in 1932. By that time the big game was plentiful enough to allow regular hunting seasons.

44

ESCAPING ANNIHILATION AT CRYSTAL CITY

Salvation with Sunshine and Eggs

Some eight torturous miles up the Crystal River from the famous Yule marble quarries in Gunnison County are the remains of Crystal City. Until about 1893 it was a community of perhaps five hundred, its mines rich in lead, zinc and silver

There it was that Ellen Jack, a rough and tumble woman, had picked and shoveled with her male employees in the mine she owned. Her autobiography, *The Fate of a Fairy*, described the many enterprises of this unique entrepreneur.

By the late 1940s war surplus jeeps enabled some summer residents to reclaim the few remaining buildings there. One, the mill of the Sheep Mountain Tunnel, hangs out over the raging waters of the river from a cliff. It is perhaps the subject of more paintings, drawings and photographs than any structure in the Colorado Rockies, being a favorite in coffee table books and calendars.

At over nine thousand feet in elevation, Crystal serves only as a summer hideaway most of the time. The deep snows would preclude year-around residence for most mortals.

In spite of this, there arrived in the autumn of 1951 a man by the name of Willis, his wife, his adopted daughter and her boyfriend. Willis was described as a sun-worshipper. He planned to establish a colony at Crystal City for people who hoped to escape annihilation of all life at less than 8,000 feet. Somehow the party had a divine revelation that this catastrophe would occur on May 12, 1952. These people were scanty in their dress, and they must have believed in the healthful benefits of eggs, as they dragged a cart of many dozen up to the town. There they had obtained a cabin.

Charlie Orlosky, a trapper at Marble, was also a deputy sheriff, and he had to arrest the boyfriend for breaking into another cabin that fall. As the first snow flew, it was noted that the pioneers had not come down from Crystal where they and their dog were apparently planning to spend the winter.

It was January when they struggled into Marble, having tramped through deep snow for five days down the precarious road, with no winter clothing, no skis, and no snowshoes. They begged Orlosky to go up and fetch their dog which they had left in the cabin. He assumed the animal had died in the bitter cold and would not risk the dangerous snowslides. The sad visionaries then went to some warmer region to spend the winter.

In early April the colonizers returned, better-clad, and headed toward Crystal City. A couple of weeks later, as Charlie was hunting, he was amazed to hear the bark of a dog coming from their cabin. It seems the animal had somehow survived the winter, living on sixteen dozen frozen eggs and a bucket of ice.

The fateful day came and went. People who lived below the designated elevation had not perished. Willis and his clan left for parts unknown. There are some who believe they destroyed the dam bridge which led to the old mill in their bitter disappointment.

45

WHEN OTTO GOT MARRIED

He Climbed Independence but Soon Gained Independence

Certainly one of the most colorful characters in the history of Western Colorado was John Otto, the eccentric man whose efforts led to the creation of Colorado National Monument.

Otto had been tried for insanity and incarcerated twice in California and tried again in Colorado before he took up residence in a cave among the monoliths which overlook Grand Junction and Fruita. His propensity for writing strange letters to public officials regarding politics, philosophy and labor laws had caused the recipients to fear he may have violent feelings against them. There was never such a tendency on Otto's part, and in each case he was released as harmless.

He had worked at various jobs in the Grand Valley, but his main crusade was that of making a park out of the spectacular formations among which he lived. Otto wrote letters to editors and officials to convince them that the area should be made into a national park. By 1911 he had succeeded in getting the designation, originally known as "Monolith National Monument," declared by the federal government.

That was soon after Beatrice Farnham, of South Weymouth, Massachusetts, was seen with him wandering the trails he had laid out in the maze of canyons. Beatrice was an artist who had been fascinated with the Far West and wore flamboyant western costumes as she traveled around making paintings of scenery. In her journeys she may have met Otto earlier, but at this time she pitched her tent near his beneath the towering Independence Rock, a sandstone monolith over five hundred feet high. Beatrice had been described as woman of great ability in art, a lady of culture.

In the spring it was announced that they were to be married. The wedding was set for June. At the same time Otto was appointed to be the custodian for the now-named Colorado National Monument with a salary of one dollar per month. Otto, who always had a flair for the dramatic, decided to drive a spike ladder up the side of the high stone pillar, so that he could scale it and plant a United States Flag atop the overhanging cap on the summit.

With much fanfare he accomplished the task, and Beatrice announced plans to found a colony for Massachusetts girls in Monument Canyon, site of the wedding. It would serve to give them a "fresh outlook" from New England upbringing.

On June 20, 1911, they were given a proper service by a Congregational pastor in the presence of friends and admirers. The only notable change in the ritual was that Otto had insisted that the words "love, honor and obey" be changed to "love, honor and cherish." After Otto had climbed Independence Rock once more to replace the large flag with a smaller one, the couple went on a honeymoon to Piñon Mesa, south of the new national monument.

Soon after they returned, Beatrice went back East to visit her family and never returned. After months of waiting, Otto admitted that they just never did get along and sued for divorce on the grounds of desertion. He was awarded $2,000 in alimony. A few years later his ex-wife married a Texas cowboy.

John Otto developed many other trails and dreamed of a rimrock drive over the monument from Grand Junction to Fruita. He promoted new roads for Grand Mesa and was the designer of the zigzag route at Land's End, which is still in use. In 1927, after a squabble over insufficient funding, he was dismissed as superintendent but later helped in the construction of rimrock drive by local workers and the Civilian Conservation Corps in 1933.

After that Otto went back to California, still writing colorful letters to those he considered influential people. He passed away in 1952, at the age of eighty-one.

46

UNSUNG HEROINES OF EDUCATION

A Donkey in the Schoolhouse

Until the establishment of a Normal School at Gunnison in 1911, Western Colorado was struggling to find teachers for isolated one-room schools in the mountains or plateaus. There were times when a girl of only seventeen who had graduated from high school was pressed into service. Her charges in the eight grades sometimes included boys older and often larger than herself. The going pay rate for teachers at these schools ranged from thirty to fifty dollars per month. Sometimes the instructor found it possible to board with nearby ranchers, but gradually the idea of a teacherage adjoining the schoolhouse was established.

There have been a myriad of accounts of such schools throughout the west, but some incidental anecdotes relative to the Western Slope bear repeating.

A graduate of the normal school found employment at Cathedral in the extreme northeast corner of Hinsdale County. One of the most isolated spots in the San Juan Mountains, Cathedral was about fourteen miles south of the settlement of Powderhorn which in turn is about half way between Gunnison and Lake City.

She wrote a letter after her first term telling her professors to emphasize resourceful planning to novices. It seems that she was marooned for nearly a week with her students because of heavy snow, too deep for riders on horseback to reach them. She advised that the teacher have a great deal of food on hand and especially have about a hundred ideas for games and crafts to keep the students occupied in such emergencies. Restless as they were under normal occasions, the confinement created massive cases of cabin fever among the children.

At Ragged Mountain School, near McClure Pass, between Paonia and Redstone, it was decided that school should be held between April and October rather than deal with severe winter conditions. On one occasion a black bear was attracted by the aroma of school lunchboxes. With a no-nonsense attitude the teacher drove the creature away with a broom.

At the Lavender School in Disappointment Valley, somewhere between Slick Rock and Bedrock, there were several times when students had to stay at the school because of high winds and drifts which made it too dangerous for them to be able to ride home on their horses.

About thirty-two miles from Gunnison was Bowerman, high in the mountains, where gold had been found. In 1904 a school was started there. Miss Edith Welch was the first teacher of some twenty students, and she was quite popular. Her successor, though, a Miss Cooper, was not so well received. Some of the boys decided to run her out by stuffing rags and gunny sacks down the stove pipe.

The fire refused to draw. Thereupon Miss Cooper called all the students in, locked the doors, opened all the windows, put on her coat, called the roll, and began the daily lessons. By recess time she announced to the shivering class that whoever had blocked the chimney might go up and pull out the rags, after which a fire would be built. They obeyed. After that, she scored a number of victories.

At a country school not far from the Black Canyon of the Gunnison, a boy had a very original idea. After everyone had left on Friday afternoon, he put a donkey into the building. This boy happened to be the son of the chairman of the Board of Education.

By Monday morning, the room was a shambles. The donkey had kicked things to pieces, and also obeyed the calls of nature all over the place. The chairman of the board declared that when the culprit was found he would be sent to the State Reformatory.

Somehow the miscreant was never identified. His secret was kept by the boy until after his father had died. A successful rancher later in life, the man believed that being sent to the reformatory would indeed have been his fate no matter if he was the son of the chairman.

47

THE OLD MAN WHO TOOK TO THE AIR

He Had a Fear of Flying

Starr Nelson was born in Indiana just a year after the end of the War Between the States, in 1866. At the age of sixteen, he was a rider on the Old Chisholm Trail, driving cattle from Austin, Texas to Abilene, Kansas. Eventually Nelson found himself in Colorado and decided to stay, homesteading in South Park.

When he was only thirty years old, he once found himself on a ledge from which the only escape was to leap thirty-six feet straight down. Starr landed on his feet, breaking both ankles and sustaining a rupture. He felt "consigned to the trash heap."

In order to support himself he went to work on the railroad, a career he held for thirty-two years. He worked up to the position of engineer, and for twenty-six years he ran a Denver and Rio Grande train over Marshall Pass.

He would end his regular run at Delta where he decided to become a rancher. This venture was a huge success, and he became a highly respected citizen, marrying and raising a family. When his beloved wife, Martha, died in 1931, Starr was grief-stricken and tended to withdraw from his many civic projects.

In 1939 Nelson decided that he needed a new challenge. He was obsessed with the idea of learning to fly. First he went to California, but authorities there decided that a man who had seen seventy-three winters was too old.

Returning home, Nelson learned that Mesa Junior College in Grand Junction offered courses in flight training. Off he went to apply. Authorities there were stunned, but they told him they would take him if he could pass the physical examination. Starr came through the medical tests in "flying colors."

In his early training the old fear possessed him. He remarked later, "My knees would tremble and my body would become rigid as glass, and I had a sensation of falling on my first flight."

By the next year, 1940, Starr Nelson became a licensed pilot. Each year he had to take another physical exam but continued for the next six years at the controls. He bought his own airplane and made a landing strip on his ranch on Ruby Mesa. By 1944 he was saluted as the world's oldest pilot. Starr walked away from a forced landing in Gunnison when a wind current blew his plane upside down.

In 1946 he flew a goodwill trip to Mexico as a guest of the Mexican government. Later that year he made a crash landing at the Grand Junction airport. His passenger, a ten year old girl, sustained only a black eye. That, however, led Nelson to give up flying.

He deeded his airport to the city of Delta. Two years later he was given a standing ovation at the National Flying Farmers' convention in Columbus, Ohio.

A year later Starr Nelson died, still holding the title as America's oldest flying farmer.

Starr Nelson is shown here with his airplane, which he flew in his seventies and eighties. Courtesy of Delta County Historical Society Museum

48

THE CAMP HALE PIPE SMOKERS
Models of Uniformity

During World War II, Camp Hale at the foot of Tennessee Pass, was the training center for the mountain and cold weather army unit known as the Tenth Mountain Division. Undergoing strenuous challenges in the high Rockies, the unit may have been a bit less formal than others. Commanding General "Snowshoe" Corlett was, however, a stickler for uniformity.

Captain Charles Barkeen was commander of Company B in that division. He was a former National Guardsman and a Denver native. He also had a fondness for his corn cob pipe.

On one inspection day he gathered his men on the parade ground in full battle dress and brought them to attention. The General did not appear when scheduled, so Captain Barkeen ordered the men to parade rest, and tired of the long wait, he took the pipe out of his pocket and lit up, the smoke spiraling above his head. Suddenly the General appeared in his jeep. Barkeen brought the company to attention but forgot the pipe in his mouth.

The general told the driver to stop and alit from the vehicle to say, "Captain, either you or your men are out of uniform. Don't let this happen again." He jumped back into the jeep and continued his inspection.

A week later the men of the company each received a corn cob pipe and a packet of tobacco, a gift of the captain. It was strongly suggested that each man have his pipe up and smoking at the next troop review. When that inspection day arrived, General Corlett noticed a substantial cloud of plume arising from Company B. There was the captain, pipe in mouth, and most of the men clenching pipes and puffing away.

Corlett stood before the Captain Barkeen and said, "That's much better!" This tended to create an esprit de corps in the unit which led to their selection as the base representative without pipes, at a Memorial Day parade in Denver.

From the 1895 Montgomery Ward Catalogue: Genuine Brier, hand carved, assorted designs or stems, genuine amber mouthpiece; an elegant pipe. Entire length, about 6 inches. Each $1.13

49

BUSTER BROWN ENDED UP IN CRAIG

The Little Boy Who Charmed All America

He was the cute little boy with whom America fell in love during the first decade of the twentieth century. In his sailor suit and with his clever dog, Tige, he traveled the nation to promote the shoes with his name, "Buster Brown."

Born in 1899 on the East Coast, Richard S. Barker was such an appealing child that the shoe manufacturer made a star attraction out of him from 1907 until 1913. With his songs, dances, clever comments and his trick dog, Buster was continually performing in cities and towns, accompanied by a tutor to see that he received a proper education.

At the age of fourteen he had to retire from show business although another youth was found to succeed him.

When the United States entered World War I, Richard enlisted and saw active duty. Upon his return from the service he married and came west looking for a ranch. It seems he had always dreamed of becoming a cowboy.

The couple found what they were looking for on the Little Snake River, about forty-five miles northeast of the town of Craig. They lived there until the early 1970s when they took up residence in Craig. He died there on December 1, 1976.

An early day Buster Brown and his dog, Tige. Buster Brown Corporation

Part Four

FOUR GREAT ESCAPES

All those discrepancies in terrain and weather or the threat of being attacked conspire to trap people in desperate situations. Perhaps the way out of such traps may be creative thought. On other occasions it is sheer endurance. Then, too, it may be a matter of simply getting away quickly. While there are numerous stories about such survival tactics, four of them have something of unique character.

50

CRAWLING TO COCHETOPA PASS

An Amazing Survival Story

During the so-called "Mormon War" in 1857 a United States Army detachment at Fort Bridger, Wyoming had lost almost all of their draft animals. The nearest source from which they could be replenished was Taos, New Mexico. Even though it was November, the necessity was so great that a unit of forty soldiers, more than a score of porters and a pack train of sixty-three mules were dispatched to cross the Continental Divide.

In charge of the expedition was Captain Randolph Marcy. Mountain men Jim Baker and Tim Goodale were retained as guides although they had never really traversed the Western Slope of Colorado. As the snows began to fall, the one Ute guide quit, claiming that to try to reach the San Luis Valley would be suicide.

Undaunted, Marcy moved southward over the Bookcliff formation near where Grand Junction is today, and then south of the Black Canyon to the Gunnison country. It was then that the snows became very deep, and Baker had no idea of where Cochetopa pass, on the Continental Divide, could be located.

Marcy related that Baker carved himself a pair of snowshoes which are today known as skis, in order to scout the region. This was the first recorded use of skis in Colorado history. The effort was of no avail as the snow was so light and deep it could not support the slats.

Snow kept falling. The mules could no longer walk and simply lay down and froze to death. Being out of all food supplies, the men cut up and ate the animal corpses. As the men's shoes wore out they tried to cover their feet with the hides of the mules. They were forced to crawl on hands and knees to get through the snow.

It was then that a lowly porter, a Mexican by the name of Miguel Alona, dared to approach Marcy with the information that he had once crossed this region and knew where the pass could be found. Skeptical, Marcy asked the guides for confirmation, but those scouts could only claim that the snow had changed the appearances so much that they could not say. Thus did Alona lead the starving party to the summit of 10,063 foot Cochetopa Pass, from which they viewed the level surface of the San Luis Valley below.

A few men who were still strong enough were sent to Fort Massachusetts, near San Luis, for food and supplies. At last these soldiers returned, and the food was devoured. One account claimed that one man ate so quickly that he died from the experience. Marcy himself had lost twenty-nine pounds.

What was supposed to be a trek of twenty-one days had lasted fifty-nine days before they reached Taos. Marcy wrote later, "I mentally offered up sincere thanks to the Almighty for delivering us from the horrible death of starvation." It was not until spring that he was able to return to Fort Bridger with the needed animals and supplies.

51

A BAREFOOT THREE HUNDRED MILE RUN

Escaping the Attack on Fort Uncompahgre

Antoine Robidoux was probably the first man to take a wagon across the Continental Divide in Colorado. This trader, one of a famous family of traders, had married the Mexican governor's adopted daughter at Santa Fe. He was then provided an exclusive right to trade with the Indians in what became Western Colorado. By 1828 Antoine had established a thriving post, Fort Uncompahgre, at the confluence of the Gunnison and Uncompahgre Rivers near the site of what is now Delta.

This was only the first of three forts he developed, the other two being in Utah. The trade, which was mutually beneficial to both the Utes and Robidoux, was to continue for sixteen years. Fort Uncompahgre was the only settlement of non-Indians in Western Colorado at that time.

Traders and trappers visited the fort frequently, and there were dealings in guns and slaves as well as the standard trading goods. In the 1840s Robidoux had established a trade system to rival that of the huge American Fur Company which was centered in Wyoming.

It was in the summer of 1843 that trouble began. Some Navajos had raided ranches west of Santa Fe. In retaliation the New Mexican government dispatched a group of volunteers to attack the Navajos. After finding no Navajos, they invaded a peaceful Ute camp, killing ten, capturing others, and stealing the livestock.

Word spread northward to the other Ute bands. In 1844 a delegation of Utes protested to authorities in Santa Fe but were met with another attack by the Mexicans. This led to an uprising among the

Indians which would reach as far north as Robidoux's Fort Uncompahgre.

At the time of the Ute attack on Robidoux's post, two employees, Jose Trujillo and Calario Cortez, were downriver checking on beaver traps. Cortez had left his outer jacket, rifle, and other gear on the river bank with Trujillo and was standing barefoot in the stream. He looked up to see his partner shot down, and realized there was a full-scale onslaught. Diving into the brush, he escaped unnoticed. When he had waded as far as the fort he came ashore cautiously and saw it was deserted with five or six bodies lying dead on the ground.

Without further hesitation Cortez sneaked up the Uncompahgre River, careful to leave no trail. When he had reached the area now known as Montrose he turned east and by a very circuitous route made his way to where the town of Gunnison is today. Continuing, he finally reached Cochetopa Pass and the San Luis Valley. Fourteen days after the attack, Cortez reached the town of Taos in New Mexico starving and barely able to walk. He had nearly frozen with no clothing except his trousers and shirt.

Considering the fact that he stayed off the trade routes and was working hard to leave no trail, it is probable that his journey was about 300 miles.

The fort was never occupied again, and two years later it was burned by the Utes. Probably the floods of the Gunnison River washed out any evidence the fort had ever existed.

A few years ago, using carefully documented descriptions, the town of Delta reconstructed the famous trading post near what must have been the original site. It is a masterpiece of authenticity. Tourists who visit the fort step back to about 1835 and will see nothing they would not have seen then, including the structures made on site, the animals, the garden vegetables, and even the people who will show them around dressed as were those who lived there long ago. It is a remarkable living history museum.

52

A CRUCIAL SKI RACE NEAR STEAMBOAT SPRINGS

Escape from a Pack of Wolves

Storm Mountain, renamed Mount Werner in 1965, overlooks the town of Steamboat Springs. Today it is the site of a huge skiing development.

It was long ago that an unknown hunter "bombed the hill" there. That was a time when skis were still called snowshoes and only one pole was used to balance and control the boards.

A trapper who had his cabin at the base of the mountain had climbed to the summit in quest of fur-bearing game on February 17, 1890. It was growing dark; he had decided to return by moonlight when he spotted a wolf which he shot.

As he was turning his seven-foot skis, he realized that a whole pack of wolves, crazed by the smell of blood from the wolf's carcass, was on the attack. One even got close enough to leap at his head, but the trapper leaned down and escaped. Then he started straight down the mountain but broke his pole in the process.

Zooming down the slope, he could barely see anything, but in a matter of moments, as he recalled, he could make out his cabin in the distance. With no pole to arrest his speed, he simply leaned over and fell down, releasing the "snowshoes" and heading home to safety. The next day he found the boards nearly a mile down the slope.

Later, he wrote of the narrow escape for the Steamboat Springs *Inter-Mountain* newspaper. It was reprinted in the *Aspen Daily Times*. While there were no witnesses, the trapper must have been subject to considerable questions, and the details of his account seemed to belie any accusation that he had made up the story.

53

STRANDED ON A MOUNTAIN LEDGE
Too Far to Jump

Perhaps every rock climber has experienced the situation in which he or she realizes that it is questionable as to whether one can reach far enough or jump to safety. It is much easier to climb up than to descend. For a time, a cold chill possesses one as the climber is not sure of the ability to escape; if there is a mistake it will mean a horrible fall and probable death.

This is the problem which faced David Lavender and his companion. A native of Telluride, Lavender knew about the proper use of rope in climbing, but in the 1930s ropes of manila hemp were heavy and cumbersome. The two men decided that on a short climb on a rock face, they would not really need a rope. They were mistaken.

On the descent they found themselves caught on a ledge with no return route. Below them was another very narrow shelf, but to try to jump to safety was out of the question. To miss even slightly would throw the victim off the face of the mountain.

The lower ledge must have been only about eight feet below them. After overcoming initial panic they devised a method which demonstrates creativity at a time of crisis.

Removing their belts, they fastened them together to girdle a protruding jutting rock beside them. Then they reluctantly removed their jeans, and tested them for strength. Tying the trouser legs together and to the belts, they were able to reach the precarious perch, from which they could escape the mountain face.

Of course, they had to leave the rescue "rope" hanging and walk trouserless for eight miles through rain-soaked underbrush to their camp. They wondered what some future climber might think when encountering the apparel hanging from an isolated ledge.

111

Lavender went on to become one of the premier historians of the American West. This was partly because he had actually been a miner and a cowboy on the family ranch near the Lone Cone above Norwood. He knew first hand the reality of the diggings, range, and also the mountain precipice.

This sketch shows just how rough some of the trails were in the San Juans. Courtesy of P. David Smith

Part Five

CREATIVE COWBOYS AND STUBBORN WOMEN

They came, they saw, and they built up or tore down. These were people who changed the wilderness into industrial and agricultural production, or simply came up with innovative ideas. They included architects, promoters, scientists, prospectors, land developers, farmers and ranchers, dam builders, skiers, quarrymen, miners of coal, and precious metals, and oil. There were also those pioneer women who simply put their feet down to get what they wanted from their ambitious menfolk.

54

LURING THE GULLIBLE

Investing in Mineral Point

Throughout early Colorado history, in both farmlands and mining camps, a great deal of the activity was promotion of real estate or absentee investment. Probably the best guide to all of this hoopla is to be found in Don and Jean Griswold's book, *Colorado's Century of "Cities"*.

Speculators were urged to send money to secure land which may or may not have access to water, to help finance mines which had not even been located or moved to what would probably become a large and prosperous city. While there are many letters and brochures which could serve as examples; those of the town of Mineral Point may suffice.

Mineral Point was located at the divide between the Animas and Uncompahgre River headwaters at an altitude of 11,475 feet in the San Juan Mountains north of Silverton. It was named for a quartz knob, found in 1873, which had yielded rich silver, but the veins were limited. It was then that the urge for more wealth and continuation of the economy led to extreme measures.

Circulated nationwide were claims that there was soon to be trolley service between the town of Animas Forks and Mineral Point. Some illustrations showed lush gardens growing at timberline. There was a picture of steamships on the Animas River! One ploy bilked investors of four million dollars to build a tunnel which never was completed.

There were occasionally some marginal pay-offs for the entrepreneurs; and in one incident, investors became rich. The Old Lout Mine was a speculation but it was the source of wealth to its promoters, who could draw money to dig a shaft 300 feet into the ground. When nothing was found, the miners were told to give up. It seems there was one more shot of dynamite left, and the last man to leave decided it might as well be used. The explosion opened one of the richest deposits of ore ever found in the district. A total of $86,000 was realized in the first month after the workers returned to the mine.

Winter conditions made the Mineral Point camp almost inaccessible, and the remote location meant huge expenses to get ore to the mills. While there may have been a population of a thousand at one time, the town began to decline quickly in the 1880s, and by the 1890s it had died.

This is the earliest known photograph of Mineral Point, probably taken about 1880.   Courtesy of P. David Smith

55

WHEN THE THUNDERING HERD CROSSED MANCOS VALLEY

The Cowboys All Returned

While most of Western Colorado was still Ute Indian territory before the uprising against Meeker by the northern bands, some settlers had been made to feel welcome by the Indians. In addition to trading goods such as pots, pans and colorful beads desired by the natives, they brought new vegetables and grain in exchange for hides, baskets, and other crafts.

Mancos Valley had a few such settlers as early as 1776, including James Radcliff and H.M. Smith. These two were eyewitnesses to a spectacular display in September of that year. First they saw a huge cloud of dust rising in the east followed by the roar of pounding hooves. Riding to a high spot, they viewed so many cattle they could not believe their eyes. All they could say was "Cows, cows and more cows!"

This was possibly the greatest cattle drive across the Western Slope in recorded history. DeMill L. Sheets, a rancher from the Greenhorn Valley of the Front Range, was herding more than 2,000 head of longhorns westward to the Blue Mountains of Utah.

Sheets did not return, but all of the cowboys who had driven the animals seemed to have become so infatuated with the pasturelands they had crossed that they came back and started ranches there themselves, helping to found the main base of economy for what would become the town of Mancos.

There are some remarkable stories about relationships between the early ranchers and the Utes. Jean Border of Mancos remembered the tales of her grandfather, one of the first settlers. He would retreat to Indian camps when caught in blizzards and was welcomed to spend as much time as needed to proceed on his way. On one occasion he became host to outlaw Utes who took refuge in his own camp.

After the official expulsion of the Utes to reservations the situation was reversed. There were violent attacks by the Indians from their newly-assigned lands, and these were met by many reprisals by the ranchers in southwest Colorado. Two decades were to pass before relative peace was restored to both the cowboys and Indians.

Enormous herds of cattle grazed on the vast plains of the West. Courtesy of P. David Smith To the Rockies and Beyond, *1879*

56

THE GREAT COLORADO LAND RUSH

The Sooners Knew Just Where to Go

According to the best estimates there were only about 5,000 Utes in what is now Colorado when the White Men began to go into the mountains seeking mineral wealth. The Utes had occupied the region of the Front Range and westward into what is now Utah. Gradually they were pushed further to the west, starting with a treaty in 1862.

By 1868 the new settlers were dealing with Ouray who was a spokesman for the Uncompahgre Utes in the southwestern segment of the state. He was able to read some in Spanish, spoke broken English, and knew the Ute dialects. He was taken to Washington, D.C., and knew of the huge number of non-Indians in the nation and their tremendous achievements in transportation, communication and weaponry. To try to convince other Utes was a difficult task. They had seen few of the "foreigners," such as traders, trappers and a few prospectors.

Whites decided Ouray could speak for all the Utes, not just his group. There were five different bands involved. Most of the others hardly recognized the spokesman who was now regarded "Chief of the Utes" for treaty purposes. In what came to be called the Kit Carson Treaty of 1868, he signed away their claim to all lands east of the 107th meridian north to the fortieth parallel. This was a north-south line just west of Gunnison, north to an east-west line north of Meeker. It excluded North, Middle and South Parks, favorite hunting grounds. Indians in those areas had no concept of the agreement and did not know anything about the lines, so they were continually "invading" white territory. After gold was discovered in the San Juan Mountains, the Brunot Treaty allowed developers into the reservation at designated sites to mine the precious metals. Then in 1879, there was the uprising in the northern section of the Ute lands which has come to be known as the Meeker Massacre; and the byword of the Denver press was, "The Utes must go!"

In one of the last acts of his life, Ouray agreed to the Ute removal which was to be to the junction of the Gunnison and Grand (Colorado) rivers, the fertile Grand Valley, where the city of Grand Junction now stands. The wording of the treaty was vague, stating "or adjoining territories." Negotiator Otto Mears persuaded Washington officials that Utah territory was "adjoining," as he was aware that the Grand Valley had the longest growing season in Colorado. Thus the Utes from the San Juans northward were to be removed to the Uintah area of Utah. Their final departure date was set for September 1, 1881. By that time, Ouray had died.

It should be borne in mind that the United States in those days was still essentially an agricultural nation. Most people were either farmers, dependent upon farm business, or related to someone who was. Growing food was in their blood, so to speak. They included the miners in such reservation towns as Ouray, Silverton and Lake City.

So how did they know that the Grand Valley had such good growing prospects for fruit? When the appointed date arrived for occupation of the former Ute lands, wagons were ready in Gunnison, Pagosa Springs, Crested Butte, Hot Sulphur Springs and Walden. It was nowhere nearly as dramatic as the Oklahoma land rush, but there was real competition to reach the best farming and ranching areas and be first to stake their claims.

Yes, there had been "sooners," those who illegally entered the promised land for speculation before the settlement date. Enos T. Hotchkiss, a Lake City mine owner, had ridden an unshod pony over to the North Fork of the Gunnison in order to deceive any Indians looking for tracks. As soon as he arrived, he laid claim to the rich land which now bears his name, Hotchkiss, Colorado. Just up the river, somehow Samuel Wade knew that chokecherries and other fruit-bearing plants were growing wild, meaning potential orchard land. When he arrived from Gunnison, he came stocked with saplings for apples and other fruits to found the town of Paonia.

Others had already known of choice lands which became Montrose, Delta and Grand Junction.

In the western part of Montrose County, it was told that in the week before the official entry, a man by the name of Gilmore was so intent on a certain piece of land that he hid in the brush for four days to escape the notice of departing Utes and the soldiers who were supposed to be looking for premature land seekers. When these men left the area, he crawled out of his hiding place. To his amazement four other men rose up from their cramped quarters. They had been hiding out with designs on the same land. After some amiable discussion, they conceded that the land should go to Gilmore as he had been hiding in the bushes for the longest time.

57

COLORADO'S CAPITOL BUILDING CAME FROM ABERDEEN

It Was a Granite Quarry in Gunnison County

The Colorado State Capitol Building at Broadway and Colfax Avenue in Denver had its origins from a hole in the ground about seven miles south of Gunnison. In 1889 Governor Job A. Cooper, responding to popular demand, established a commission to select a stone which could be used to build a proper and functional center of government for Colorado.

Land on the hill overlooking downtown Denver had been donated by Henry C. Brown. Granite from the Aberdeen Quarry was chosen for its uniformity and flawlessness. It was necessary that the railroad build a branch to the diggings in order to transport some of the largest blocks of granite ever quarried up to that time, some as much as fifteen tons.

A small community was established with a rooming house and dining room for fifty workers. At the outset they labored ten hours a day, seven days a week, in order to supply the shipments to Denver. Denver, it seems, was a bit tardy on its end, and Gunnison threatened to build the structure on its own turf. Several towns in the state had designated "capitol hills" with an eye toward stealing the governance from Denver.

At last the Queen City was ready with 139 cutters and forty other workers at the site. They complained to their union about the demanding hours and were soon accommodated. This inspired the Aberdeen crew to go on strike. They had been shipping twenty carloads of granite a day. An attempt to replace them was a disaster.

Using unemployed cowboys, hobos and other unskilled workers, the operation went to pieces. In one week the strikebreakers were able to quarry only four carloads. The strikers were victorious. The working hours were cut to only nine hours a day at the same pay, and they were given Sundays off.

Two men died in the operation of the granite removal. A Swede was crushed to death and another man, injured from a broken derrick boom died months later. The wife of the bookkeeper succumbed to pneumonia she acquired in the frigid climate.

By 1894 the capitol building was completed. While the quarry continued to supply a few other structures, the railroad tore up its tracks, and stone had to be carried out in wagons. Enough extra granite was taken out to supply some repairs and additives to the Denver structure, but that was about all that proved financially feasible. Before long there were only a few rotting buildings and a deep hole left.

58

THOSE "DOBES" NEAR CRAWFORD

A Legacy of "Diamond Joe"?

A long a county road north of the town of Crawford, there are some barren hills locally referred to as the "Dobes". This term refers to the adobe clay that tops them, with no topsoil to grow grass. While it cannot be proven beyond possible doubt, early settlers claimed that those hills were covered with lush growths of grass until John D. Morrisey showed up.

Morrisey had cashed in on the Leadville silver boom of the early 1880s with financing from a Mississippi gambler called "Diamond Joe" Reynolds. John was illiterate and was somehow victimized by his secretary, losing his mines as well as the favor of his benefactor.

Not to be defeated, Morrisey adopted the name of "Diamond Joe" himself and was able to borrow enough from other miners to invest in a very large herd of cattle. The former Ute reservation lands had just been opened up, and Morrisey knew that Leadville and other mining camps would be ready markets for fresh beef.

Thus it came to pass that he homesteaded a ranch which he called the Diamond Joe and ran a fantastic number of cattle on the land. Some claim he had as many as thirty thousand head on an area that should not have supported more than a few thousand. He knew nothing of ranching, much less of the responsibilities of grazing.

Without raising hay for winter feeding, he simply let the cattle graze wherever they might throughout the year. The bovines ate the grass to the very roots leaving the topsoil victim to rains and melting snows which washed it away exposing the barren adobe.

The operation of the ranch lasted only a couple of years from 1882 until a devastating winter of 1884 starved off most of the herd.

Morrisey, once again financially destitute, returned to Leadville and tried to manage mines once more. This time he fell under the influence of John Barleycorn and died in the Lake County poorhouse.

He was once asked how he could have gone broke after attaining a fortune and is said to have replied, "I spent my money on horses, gambling, women and whiskey. The rest I wasted."

The work of the Telluride pinheads allowed local mines to use AC current very soon after its inventions. Courtesy of P. David Smith

59

THE TELLURIDE PINHEADS

Their Studies Were Electrifying

When the Gold King Mill, located at 12,000 feet elevation above Telluride, ran out of trees to feed its direct electric power plant, it had to switch to coal. The expense of getting coal was so high that the company, under the direction of L. L. Nunn, was faced with bankruptcy.

Nunn conceived the idea of a water-powered plant which could produce alternating current and transmit it to the mines. The concept had been demonstrated on a limited scale by the famous scientist Nicholas Tesla, and George Westinghouse had experimented with alternating current power in a small way. Thomas Edison claimed it would never work. When Nunn convinced Westinghouse that a power plant at Ames, almost three miles from the Gold King, could provide electricity, Westinghouse undertook the financing.

The plant was constructed, and by 1890 it was able to transmit a hundred horsepower with 3,000 volts over that distance with a power loss of less than five per cent. Not only were the mines saved from financial disaster, but the town of Telluride became the first in the world to have A-C lighting. Expenses for the Gold King's electricity dropped from $2,500 to $500 per month.

Nunn's brother, P.N. Nunn, was the engineer who built the Ames plant. He soon realized, however, that there were no schools in the nation which taught courses in alternate current electrification. With a personal donation from Westinghouse, he established what eventually came to be known as the Telluride Institute. A score of talented young technicians came for two years of training. The foundation paid them thirty dollars a month in addition to room and board. Both classroom instruction and field training were included.

Why they were called "pinheads" by local residents has not been revealed; perhaps it was a colloquial expression now referring to nerds or eggheads. In any event, they impressed the citizenry when, threatened with a flood from a broken dam, they used slide rules to calculate that the waters would not quite reach their plant. The engineers remained calm as the flood reached exactly the level predicted.

Over the years, L. L. Nunn acquired property at Olmstead, Utah, and the Institute was moved there. As it became more in demand, by 1910 he built an impressive "Telluride House" at Cornell University in Ithaca, New York, and that is still the site of the Telluride Institute. Whether its students are still called "pinheads" is doubtful.

Nunn was a true philanthropist. In later life he was an educational innovator. He founded a school named Deep Springs at a ranch in Inyo County, California. It was developed on the idea of individual self-help and creative license for talented teenagers and has acquired a worldwide reputation.

60

DELTA WOMEN WIELDED THEIR POWER

Only Sandwiches for Supper

Women did not have a vote in public matters back in the 1880s, but that did not mean they couldn't decide a great deal in town politics.

For instance, the Delta Federated Women's Club became concerned over the common drinking ladle used in the school at a time when tuberculosis victims were arriving to take the cure in Western Colorado. They hassled the men's clubs until they got a water fountain. Then they set out on a campaign to stop trash being thrown into the dirt streets and persuaded the town to set up trash barrels.

Most annoying to the ladies were the boardwalks. These caught their heels, snagged their dresses, and were so uneven as to cause tripping. The club members confronted the town fathers about this matter. No money was available, they were told, and the streets would have to be paved if sidewalks were laid. No one wanted higher taxes to finance such ambitious dreams.

The dirt streets were dusty in the summer, and in the springtime so muddy that a loaded wagon could sink to its hubs.

Then came the revolution in the form of a realization. Most of the men in power were the husbands of members of the club. The ladies got into violent agreement that they would stand together on a plan to realize their goal.

No more of the excellent evening meals would be served until the men agreed to build sidewalks and pave the streets. Only small sandwiches would be offered to the hungry town power brokers. Suddenly money was found to finance the projects and Delta had sidewalks.

That wasn't the end of their campaigns. They were sick of seeing men spit tobacco juice on the new sidewalks. The local brickyard was pressured into scoring bricks with the message "Don't Spit" to be placed into the sidewalks.

Their efforts would continue after that, including the founding of a library and a number of cultural enrichment programs.

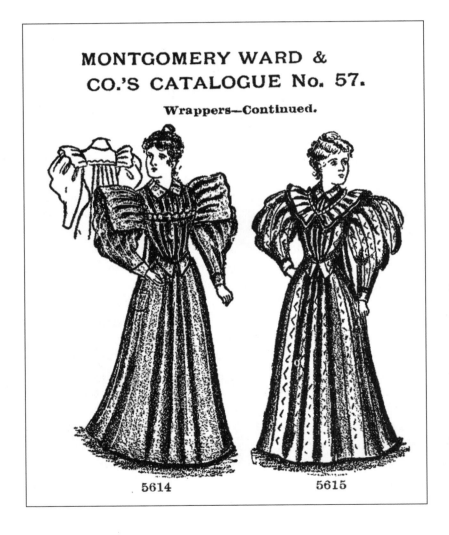

MONTGOMERY WARD & CO.'S CATALOGUE No. 57.

Wrappers—Continued.

5614   5615

61

DISCOVERING THOSE STONES THAT BURNED

Mike Callahan's Fantastic House-Warming

Early-day trappers and traders usually got along quite well with the Ute Indians of Western Colorado. They often shared campfire stories. One of the mountain men related a story of the Indians tossing what seemed to be an ordinary rock, not coal, into the campfire, where it burst into flames.

Among the early settlers along the Grand River (now named the Colorado River), near where the town of Parachute is located, was James Robinson Mass. He built a cabin there and constructed a rock fireplace. When he lit a fire and saw the stones begin to ooze a black substance he ceased using the fireplace.

Not so wary was Mike Callahan. He constructed his cabin with available materials, and then invited his friends to a housewarming. The fire was lit, but the fireplace rock started to burn, and the entire cabin was razed by the flames. A mountain near Parachute is named in his memory.

These rocks were oil shale. In 1888 H. W. Hallett had settled in that region and had a visit from his brother who lived in Springfield, Massachusetts. The brother learned about the shale from Indians who still wandered into the territory. He took a big pipe and pounded it full of the rock. Then he placed a drain at the bottom of the pipe and heated it red hot. The pipe ran out a full quart of oil which he took home to Springfield with him, but apparently did nothing with the discovery.

As time went on, dreams of a new source of oil began to excite the residents of the valley. In 1917, using diagrams from a copy of the *Encyclopedia Britannica*, Harry Flynn of DeBeque constructed an oil shale retort modeled after one used in Scotland. The Scotch shale was different from the Colorado shale, as it turned out, and the costs were too high for the profitable extraction of the fuel.

In the ensuing decades, there were a number of flurries of excitement over the possibilities of oil shale development. Several companies were founded and went bankrupt trying to produce oil that was competitive with well production. Author and playwright Dalton Trumbo constantly referred to Grand Junction as "Shale City" in his works.

After World War II, the most outspoken promoter of oil shale development was Tell Ertl. As chief of the mining section of the United States Bureau of Mines, he was instrumental in the construction of an experimental plant near Rifle. He was department chairman of mining and petroleum at Ohio State University and prospected many claims himself. With oil shale beds underlying an estimated 16,500 square miles of Colorado, Utah and Wyoming, Ertl realized this was more potential oil than had been used in all of American history. Some people believed he was the inspiration for a major character in Ayn Rand's famous novel, *Atlas Shrugged*.

It was not until the critical oil shortages of the 1970s that the nation became alarmed. The United States Government established subsidies for the production of oil shale with the leading recipient being Exxon Corporation. Five billion dollars were put into development within a short time. It was the greatest boom Western Colorado had ever experienced.

By the 1980s, 21,000 people were involved in oil shale production, and prosperity was rife from Grand Junction to Glenwood Springs. New luxury hotels were built along Horizon Drive in Grand Junction; a whole new city, Battlement Mesa, was being constructed by Exxon across the river from Parachute.

As the subsidies dwindled, and still the price of production was not competitive, a major decision was reached in the plush offices of Exxon in New York City. On May 2, 1982, which would be called "Black Sunday" throughout west central Colorado, Exxon announced discontinuance of the program. Other companies followed suit, and the Western Slope was thrown into the worst financial depression in its history. Those expensive hotels were competing with budget hostelries for customers. With the loss of those 21,000 jobs, related service businesses went bankrupt, and property values plunged, as hundreds of owners walked away from new homes, unable to keep up mortgage payments.

It was not until a decade later that the first signs of recovery occurred, but they were not in oil shale production.

Grand Junction about 1980 with mountains of shale in the background. Courtesy of Jim Du Bois

62

CUISINE AT THE BLACK CANYON HOTEL

Recycled T-bones?

At the village of Cimarron, near what is now the massive Morrow Point Dam, the Black Canyon Hotel was a popular stop on the narrow-gauge railroad. That was when the Denver and Rio Grande Railway had a line through part of the canyon between Gunnison and Montrose, pulling out of the depths at that point. In the early 1900s, the hotel was a popular lunch stop and was most noted for its fresh salads and tasty desserts.

Another feature of the hotel was the amazingly low price it charged for T-bone steaks. It was later revealed that the kitchen workers would take round steaks, cut them to proper shape, and then pound a T-bone into the meat. Of course, after the meal had been eaten, the bone could be removed and used again and again.

63

BUSY DAYS ON THE UINTAH LINE

When a Building Load of Bricks was Mailed by Parcel Post

Mack, a town eleven miles from the Utah border in Mesa County, was established in 1903 along the Denver and Rio Grande Railway. It was the anchor point for the unique Uintah Railway over Baxter Pass to Dragon, Utah. Mack was named for the president of the Barber Asphalt and Paving Company of New Jersey. That corporation owned a huge gilsonite mine, one of only two in the world at that time. Gilsonite was used in asphalt, paints, roofing and printers' ink; later it would become a source of gasoline.

Most of the fifty-three-mile line was in Mesa, Garfield and Rio Blanco counties and entered Utah for a few miles. Completed in 1904, the line was later extended eleven miles to the town of Watson, Utah. While designed to supply needed materials to Dragon and haul ore out, it was also a postal route which served Vernal, Utah, and Rangely, Colorado, through its own express wagons. A section of the railroad zigzagged over Baxter Pass on a seven per cent grade called by some the "crookedest railroad in the West."

In 1915 the Bank of Vernal decided to build a brick structure. The bricks were to be brought in from Salt Lake City, 175 miles away. Freight prices were $2.50 per hundred pounds, but parcel post was only $1.05 for the same weight. Vernal officers decided to have the bricks mailed from Salt Lake City to Mack, then continue on the Uintah to Watson, and thence by Uintah Wagon Express to Vernal, Utah.

Each brick was wrapped separately in paper, and they were packed in cartons of fifty pounds each. There was a great deal of back-breaking labor at the Mack terminal, transferring each box for shipment to Watson. It was merciful that the entire supply was sent out

133

gradually, but finally there were enough bricks in Vernal to build the bank which opened in 1916. Although the name has changed, and the structure has been enlarged; it still stands at Main Street and Vernal Avenue.

When the post office at Mack complained, the postal department set a limit of 200 pounds daily maximum for parcel post; that was later reduced to only fifty pounds.

As for the plucky little railroad, it continued until 1939 when it was replaced by a pipeline to carry crushed gilsonite to a refinery near Fruita. The gilsonite corporation changed hands several times.

This is the area of northwest Colorado where the Great Cricket War took place. Courtesy of Edward F. Carpenter

64

THE GREAT CRICKET WAR

Building Tin Walls

They were known as Mormon crickets because they were first noted in 1847 when they attacked the farms of the Salt Lake City pioneers. Members of the Latter-day Saints who had settled in Utah had planted their crops. They looked forward to a successful harvest when they were beset by "countless millions" of crickets. These two-inch long insects were related to katydids and devoured everything in range, both vegetable and animal. Females would lay up to 200 eggs before they moved on. Praying for deliverance, the Mormons were blessed with the arrival of flights of sea gulls from the lake. The birds swooped down and devoured the dreaded orthopterons. There is a monument to the sea gulls in Temple Square.

That was not the last invasion of the destructive insects. They appeared from time to time, usually to meet the same fate. However, at least two times the horde reached the Colorado border, crawling like a great carpet across the deserts in Garfield, Rio Blanco and Moffat Counties. There was no large body of water to attract gulls. No other apparent natural enemies could stay the progress of this vast army in its relentless march, miles wide in some places.

A major invasion of Brown's Park, in the northwestern corner of the state, devoured the grazing lands and marched through parts of Moffat and Routt Counties in 1927 and 1928. Farmers tried to make noise with pots, pans, tin buckets and horns to scare the vile plague of locusts, but to no avail. The pests were said to thrive on a spray of arsenic and lime which was used to eliminate them. Turkeys were sent by the carload from Denver. The gobblers ate until they became ill, probably from the poison. The turkeys rolled over dying, and were devoured by the crickets.

Finally tin fences, fifteen inches high and three inches into the ground, were strung across the territory. Some of these were two and one-half miles in length. The wooden props to hold them up had to be on the protected side, or the critters would climb up them and fall over the barrier. The tin was slanted inward, facing the crickets. There were monitored, tin-lined pits, two feet deep and four feet wide, at intervals where the insects, trying to get around the fences would fall. They could not crawl out of these, but there were plenty of other crickets to fill the holes. According to Farrington Carpenter, who witnessed this, the pits were watched 24 hours a day, by campfires at night. When the pits started to fill, gasoline was poured in, killing "billions" of them. A rattlesnake which fell into the pit was eaten to a skeleton in a short time. The fences worked!

A decade later, the destroyers moved into the Rangely area, headed toward Blue Mountain. By this time the paved highways had signs warning motorists to beware of the mass of locusts crossing their paths as drivers could lose control and skid off the road.

That time there was a local Civilian Conservation Corps unit, a New Deal employment program, stationed nearby. Mobilized, they knew what to do, erecting the long tin fences and pits. This salvation of the hay fields was a welcome sight when drought had impoverished the farmers and ranchers. At last there had been rain, and the Mormon crickets had been stopped. The wars were over.

65

SKIMMING OVER THE CONTINENTAL DIVIDE

The Eaglerock Aeroplane Was Overloaded

There had been some stunt fliers and parachutists over towns in Western Colorado early in the twenties, but they were daredevils. Most of them were veteran pilots of World War I, barnstorming all over the nation, landing in any field large enough to handle their machines (then still called aeroplanes.)

In 1928 the community of Montrose decided to build an airfield on nearby Sunset Mesa. This was not very fancy but had four dirt landing strips which came together at a point where a big circle was marked for air viewing.

The people in Montrose and surrounding counties became enamored of the idea of air mail service. It was announced that there would be air mail flown from the airfield to Pueblo, to connect with Denver. Citizens crowded the post offices to buy five-cent air mail stamps for the first flight.

Local bush pilot Walt Piele had the contract. He owned an Eaglerock with a World War I motor, water-cooled. When it came time to stow the cargo, he was not at all happy with the load of 360 pounds. It seemed that everyone wanted to send a letter on the initial flight. His plane was designed to hold only 200 pounds of cargo in addition to the pilot.

Not wanting to disappoint the many who showed up to watch him take off, he decided to give it a try. Just barely clearing a barbed-wire fence at the end of the field, Piele was airborne.

Gradually, the plane gained altitude, and flew smoothly enough over the town of Gunnison. When the pilot reached Doyleville, though, he realized that he would never clear Monarch Pass at 11,312 feet elevation.

That's when he decided on a radical idea. Near that village towers Tomichi Dome, something of a huge geological bubble formation, about which many earth scientists become excited. It rises to 10,200 feet, nearly a half mile above the valley floor. Piele began to fly around and around it to gradually gain the altitude needed. When he reached the highest point he knew he would have enough lift to clear the pass. . . . barely.

Making it over the gap on the Continental Divide, he began the descent on the eastern side, but by then, because of the extra circuits he had made, he saw that the fuel gauge was running very low. He then glided into a field spotted near Poncha Springs, west of Salida, and made a safe landing.

Walt got out and walked to the home of a very excited and rather proud farmer and telephoned a Salida filling station. Before long, a truck arrived with a barrel of gasoline and as many curious people as the van could carry. The craft would need every drop of the fuel. Once again the pilot was faced with a problem. Could he get airborne once more? Well-wishers helped him roll the plane to the farthest corner of the field, and once more he was able to take off with his heavy load. The rest of the journey was merely a matter of flying down the Arkansas River to Pueblo where the mail was transferred to a regular carrier.

66

A SURE-FIRE REAL ESTATE
DEAL ALMOST FAILED

Frisco's First Subdivision

Things were pretty slow in the town of Frisco in 1930, so slow that people just moved out to try to find employment elsewhere. That's when Bill Thomas found that although he had a ranch adjoining the village, there were not enough people left to buy the milk, butter and cream which he produced from his milk cows.

Then came a thought wave. He scoured the Denver newspapers for names of people he thought might have the wherewithal to desire a mountain homesite. William wrote a hundred letters offering choice segments of his ranch at no cost at all to each of these people. Only two responses arrived. If a deal sounds too good to be true, it probably is.

One response came from a Kansas man who had merely heard about it second hand. The other interested party was the Reverend Robert D. Dexheimer of Denver.

Dexheimer took his family up to Frisco, had a "look-see", and realized the offer was not a bogus bait. He selected a site. Then he told his congregation about the offer. Soon others took up the sites. Rough summer cabins were built, and within a short time, Thomas had neighbors to buy his products.

Today those sites are valuable properties. As for Thomas, a worthless ranch had turned into a profitable business deal, after all.

67

THOSE OLD ROCKS AT A DURANGO CAFE

Gold or Merely Fools' Gold?

During the days of the Great Depression of the 1930s, there were quite a few unemployed young men who showed up in Colorado hoping to find precious metals. Most of these prospectors had only a rudimentary idea of what formations might bear gold or silver.

When a husky, clean young man stopped in at Newton's Cafe in Durango, he started visiting with the proprietor. He claimed that, while not experienced, he knew quite a bit about rock and mineral identification. What he needed was a grubstake: pick, shovel, food and other supplies. In such an arrangement the person supplying the goods is entitled to half the ownership of any discovery. In most cases nothing of value is found, although there have been some remarkable exceptions.

Mr. Newton was persuaded that this ambitious prospector was deserving of a chance, so he supplied the goods, and the youth set out on his quest. Two weeks later, the elated young man came running in with a number of spectacular rocks he had dug from his incipient mine.

Both were thrilled with the find which sparkled in brilliant gold colors. A more experienced miner in the cafe dashed their hopes when he laughed at the ore samples. They were not gold, but iron pyrite, or so-called "fools' gold."

Indeed, iron pyrite crystals look more like gold than does the gold-bearing, dull surfaced ore itself. Many an amateur has had moments of excitement in panning until the flash in his pan turned out to be pyrite.

The disheartened young argonaut disappeared and never came back to claim the rocks. Newton believed they were pretty enough to serve as a decoration and put them on a shelf in the dining room. One day an experienced mining engineer was looking at the specimens and remarked that they seemed likely to contain silver and gold in addition to the pyrite.

Doubtful, Newton decided it would do no harm to have the samples assayed. They were judged to be worth $5,000 a ton! Alas, the discoverer and the only person who knew where they had been found could not be located. Newton was left half owner of a mine which might have yielded millions of dollars, but he never found out where it was.

These early day prospectors were also looking to strike it rich. Courtesy of P. David Smith

68

COLORADO'S MOST ELABORATE SKI TOW

It Only Lasted One Day

In 1938 three Gunnison men devised an idea for a ski tow which has no known parallel in Colorado history. It was only two years after the first ski lift in the state had been built at Berthoud Pass, but that one was only a rope tow. Wes McDermott, Rial Lake and Charles Sweitzer, three avid members of the Gunnison Ski Club, chartered a train on the narrow gauge line between Gunnison and Salida.

This line crossed the Continental Divide at Marshall Pass, 11,312 feet above sea level. The train took 137 skiers to the top of the pass. They could then glide down 700 feet. The train, meantime, backed down to the Shawano siding at the bottom of the run. It would pick up the skiers for a comfortable, heated, plush-seated ride up to the summit for another run.

The locomotive made the trip back and forth all day, except when it had to make way for the regularly-scheduled Denver and Rio Grande trains which ran between Montrose and Salida. Alas, this expensive mode of transportation lasted only one day.

The festivities were joined by expert ski maker Thor Groswald. T. J. Flynn, who would soon try to develop a ski resort at Ashcroft, near Aspen, also came over to join the fun. A third dignitary was Count Phillipe de Pret, a world-renowned master of the sport, who was then the resident instructor at Colorado Springs' famed Broadmoor Hotel. Novices who sought to learn the sport had ideal tutoring in the art of skiing by de Pret, who did not charge for his services but luxuriated in the fine appointments of the special chartered ski lift.

142

69

THE GREAT GARMESA EXPERIMENT

Quaker Oats' Model Ranch

About fifteen miles north of the town of Fruita, the Quaker Oats corporation undertook a project which was to prove that with modern equipment, a model farming community could thrive without the benefit of general irrigation systems or adequate rainfall. Straddling the Mesa and Garfield county lines, the ranch was named Garmesa. It was founded in 1911.

The site was just beneath the Bookcliff formation which overlooks the Grand Valley. Quaker Oats built a reservoir of twenty-one acres to supply water to the twenty families who would live in the subsidized housing to operate the ranch. A distillery was built to supply good drinking water to each of the houses.

Barns were heated, and water was piped into each stall for the livestock which included highbred cattle, sheep and hogs. Cork floors were placed in the pig barns to assure more efficient sanitation. Grain storage bins over fifty feet deep were made of concrete. A mansion was built for the manager, Robert Lazear, a son-in-law of one of the Crowell family which controlled Quaker Oats.

Even motorized equipment was furnished in those early days of the automobile. Tractors were used to plant various crops including, of course, oats. An orchard was established to grow fruits which could be marketed.

Even though the total yearly precipitation was about eight inches, the plan was to demonstrate that modern technology could compensate for desert conditions. A school was built, and recreation facilities were established.

Generally, the colony functioned as hoped. By 1918 a prize-winning bull from Garmesa was the feature of the state fair. The orchard had not yet begun to furnish the fruits of the labor.

Gradually the loose soils of the Bookcliffs began to silt up the reservoir, and less water was obtained. By 1920 the project was discontinued, and the company sought a new site for experiments in Wyoming.

A few diehard residents remained until the 1930s, but finally the homes were torn down or moved into the valley below. Today only a few concrete foundations may be found among the sagebrush which has recovered its domain.

This postcard showing a Grand Valley fruit orchard is postmarked 1911. Courtesy of P. David Smith

70

INUNDATED AND BURIED ALIVE

These Were Not Yet Ghost Towns

Before the Dillon Dam was built in 1961 thousands of travelers stopped at the Wildwood Lodge in the town of Dillon. That was where Highway 6 met Highway 9. This was the closest restaurant to formidable Loveland Pass, before the Eisenhower Tunnel was dug. There, eastbound travelers would stop to check equipment or ask about the weather on the pass. Some westbound truckers, concerned about fellow drivers, would make inquiries of other travelers as to whether they had spotted some other rig that may have jackknifed or been caught in a snowdrift up above.

Now Wildwood and the original town of Dillon lie beneath the waters of Dillon Reservoir. It had been an important ranching and mining town in the days when the Denver and South Park Railroad ran through that region on its Leadville route. During the years of the Great Depression, the Denver Water Board began to buy up homesites and other properties at very low prices from owners who could no longer pay the taxes. In the years following World War II, the town's population declined to eighty. Those residents were informed they would have to move the town and its cemetery, which had a greater population of 327. The modern Dillon stands on the hill that overlooked the original community.

Another town which was taken by that lake was the tiny community of Dickey, a former rail center for the valley.

At about the same time, the town of Sapinero, which stood at the junction of the Gunnison River and its Lake Fork, west of Gunnison, also had to move uphill, cemetery and all. This was to provide space for the waters of Blue Mesa Reservoir, the lake with the longest shoreline in Colorado. Another town beneath that lake, Iola, was a railroad stop between Sapinero and Gunnison.

As early as 1943, Green Mountain Dam had been constructed further down the Blue River from Dillon. As the waters behind it filled, they inundated the entire town of Lakeside, a ranching community which had once stood beside a smaller natural lake in Summit County.

Also in that county was what remained of Monarch, once a thriving lumbering town and later a resort. There had been a large box factory there, and for a time there was a railroad running from Granby to Monarch. It later became a popular summer resort known as Ka Rose. When the massive Colorado-Big Thompson Transmountain Water Diversion project was completed after World War II, the waters of Lake Granby flowed over what was once Ka Rose. Nearby, not disturbed, is the idyllic Monarch Lake.

Deeply entombed beneath the tailings of the Climax Molybdenum Mine on Fremont Pass are the sites of Kokomo and Robinson, which at one time rivaled Leadville in silver production, and had populations in the thousands. It was in Kokomo that Arthur Redman Wilfley invented the Wilfley Table which revolutionized gold mining worldwide by making the recovery of that mineral more efficient.

By 1966 the output of tailings was filling the scenic upper Ten Mile Creek valley where these two towns were located. Cemeteries were moved uphill, but the towns were purchased and burned by Climax Mine before the sludge, which has become an infamous landmark, moved in.

71

BOATING DOWN FROM THE MINE

Innovative Transportation at Bowie

About five miles up the North Fork of the Gunnison River from Paonia is the former mining town of Bowie. High above it on a steep grade is the entrance to the coal mine. Workers there would have a hard climb up to work each day and then have to watch their steps as they made their way back down.

To transport equipment and coal, a rail tramway was built up the forty-five degree slope. In 1908, miner Eugene Frank had an idea. Working at his home, Frank designed a wooden boat with a single groove on the underside which would just fit over one rail of the tramway.

On this, a miner could sit, cross his legs, and place his lunch pail between them. His left arm would reach over to hold an outrig on the other rail; his right could press on a brake made from rubber hose.

After work, a miner could climb aboard and coast down the steep slope. It could then be hauled up for the next passenger. Not only did the ride save lots of trudging after a hard day at work, but it was more fun than any amusement park ride.

The Bowie mine stopped production in the early 1970s and was sold to the Adolph Coors Company of Golden. The new owners donated much of the heavy equipment from the mine to the State Historical Society where it is on display at the Colorado Heritage Museum in Denver's Civic Center.

72

MYTHICAL STRUCTURES

Two-Story Outhouses and a Ten-Story Sun Building

Visitors to the town of Crested Butte are sometimes shown what are purported to be two-story outhouses. There is usually a very heavy layer of snow, measuring six feet or more in depth during the winter. There is an implication that when the snow is so deep, the second floor is used.

This folk story is ridiculous, of course. Can one even imagine what the first story might look like when the snow melts? Nevertheless, there are high, narrow structures in the back-yards of several homes, with doors high up on them. They are smoke houses for the preparation of game sausage. There is only one outhouse with two off-set heights in the town.

During the height of the uranium boom in Grand Junction in 1959, a major news magazine had an article describing the fantastic Sun Building under construction there. It was to be a ten-story building on some sort of a central swivel and could turn 360 degrees to take advantage of the sun. It would shade offices during the hot summer days and gradually, as the position of the sun changed, it would take advantage of the winter warmth of sunlight. One business journal published a picture of it as if it were already in existence. The structure would appear to float on a pond surrounding it. Some practical Britishers were wondering how the plumbing was handled.

No Sun Building was ever built. The uranium boom became a bust, and the corporation planning never proceeded with any construction at all.

73

RANGELY FIELD GETS AN INJECTION

Gas Pushes the Oil up

There were some shallow oil reservoirs known in the Rangely field as early as 1876, but no attempts to reclaim the lubricant were undertaken before the turn of the century. Even then such recovery was slight. It was not until 1931, with Chevron's "Raven A 1" well, 6335 feet deep, that the extent of the underground "liquid gold" was realized, now one of the biggest oil fields in the Rocky Mountains, having produced well over 750 million barrels of petroleum.

What is known as the Weber Sand Reservoir in Rio Blanco County covers 20,000 acres. The oil layer varies from only a few feet to 850 feet in thickness more than a mile below the sagebrush-strewn surface.

As a part of the underground pool was depleted, water was pumped down so the oil could float closer to the surface. Beginning in 1986 carbon dioxide (CO_2) was added to the injection, which forced the oil to rise with more intensity. The CO_2 is piped in from Wyoming, and both are recycled at the Rangely site.

The resulting pure crude oil is then piped to a Salt Lake City refinery for processing into gasoline. It is estimated that there are still some two hundred million barrels of recoverable fuel in the field.

74

THE HARE-KRISHNA COWBOYS

They Also Made Candy

Many people think of the Hare-Krishna religious group in terms of their colorful robes, shaved heads with a pony tail, and their solicitation of funds in airports throughout the United States. Some think the Hindu cult originated in India, but the sect was founded in America, and was not introduced to Asia until the 1970s.

According to ancient Hindu beliefs, Krishna was the ninth incarnation of the god, Vishnu, or "the preserver." In the classic book, *The Bhagaavad-Gita,* he became the being who reveals the message which is similar in many ways to the Christian Sermon on the Mount. Krishna was a cow-herder, and had a revelation regarding the sacred nature of all animals which led to the widespread custom of vegetarianism in India.

During the turbulent 1960s, when many American youth had come to question the beliefs of their elders, they sought alternate methods to express their religious feelings, and thus was the Hare-Krishna movement born. One branch of the organization was the International Society of Krishna Consciousness of Colorado with its headquarters in Denver.

A leader there was the charismatic and efficient manager, Bruce Webster. He secured a contract from the U.S. Forest Service for the group to cut beetle-killed timber on the Front Range of the Colorado Rockies. Thus, the members were able to earn enough money to buy a ranch property on Sunshine Mesa, two and a half miles northwest of the town of Hotchkiss in Delta County.

In 1978 they bought 360 acres adjoining the ranch of Bill Lemoine. There were some forty or fifty members of the group. They bought cattle, but since they were vegetarians they would not raise them for slaughter, but rather use the dairy products from their jersey heifers. They castrated the bulls and tried to train them as oxen, but with very little success, according to Lemoine.

It seems that during that era of predicted severe energy shortage in America, the Krishnas saw economic collapse in the offing and recognized a need to return to traditional survival methods in the future.

Some of the members founded the Bliss Bar factory in Hotchkiss where they manufactured and marketed several types of granola-based candy bars. This endeavor was operated in an old creamery building. Krishnas worked on the sweets to the tune of loudspeaker chants which could be heard up and down the town's main street.

Living arrangements on the ranch consisted of a number of mobile homes in addition to the ranch house. The "cowboys" often consulted Lemoine for advice. They were upset over his raising of Charolais cattle until he explained that they were for breeding, not slaughter. When one of their own cattle died, they held an elaborate funeral service, burying the deceased in a new tarp. There was also dismay about the presence of prairie dogs, and they did not appreciate the problem until their neighbor pointed out that the rodents hosted the infamous bubonic plague. This could be a serious threat to their children. What they wanted, according to Lemoine, was a "Pied Piper" to lead the varmints off. This problem was never resolved.

Work on the ranch was voluntary, but under the leadership of Webster, the operation went remarkably well for several years. The director was well-versed in irrigation methods and policies.

Some conservative Hotchkiss residents were upset at the presence of this strange religious group, believing them to be using illegal drugs, although that practice was absolutely forbidden in the discipline of the faith. Some local hoodlums would occasionally go up and disturb the cattle. In one incident, a dead hog was left on the road in front of the ranch.

Lemoine had to help them out in dealing with some practical problems which the Lord Krishna seemed to leave to the followers' own initiative. Compromises had to be made as insects ate their alfalfa as well as that of the non-believers. Nevertheless, dreams soared, and the Krishnas felt the time would come when they could build a shrine as their religious center.

Alas, the control by Webster became too complex, and the responsibilities had to be too widely distributed. By 1984 the sect could no longer make payments on the mortgage and went into foreclosure. Thus the Krishna Consciousness departed the valley as abruptly as it had arrived six years earlier.

Early day cowboys had other uses for cattle besides eating them. Courtesy of P. David Smith, Frank Leslie's Newspaper, *May 5, 1888*

75

COLORADO'S CANNY CANINE CONVENTION
Meeker's Classic Sheepdog Championships

Every September border collies from all over North America come to Western Colorado for the Meeker Classic Sheepdog Championship Trials. This event, started in 1987, has become the largest and most prestigious contest in America. As many as 136 entrants with their dogs arrive to herd sheep, most of whom have never encountered a dog before, through a series of intricate maneuvers.

On a meadow at least as large as four football fields, the handler stands in one spot and gives commands either by a whistle or by voice. His or her dogs rush to the far end of the field and circle the sheep. They never touch the animals—even to give a threatening nip. Crouching on command, they drive the sheep in as straight a line as possible toward the handler and then begin a number of almost amazing moves.

Listening to such signals as move clockwise or counter-clockwise, gather the flock, come straight in, or stop, the dogs run the sheep through various narrow gates and into a central circle. Then, so ordered, they will separate two or three sheep with red collars from their companions.

Finally, the collies must herd the ovine bevy into a corral. While the handler may open and close the gate, he is not permitted to have any contact with the sheep themselves. Only the clever dogs may herd them in.

As many as ten thousand spectators have shown up to view the spectacle over a four-day program of eliminations and championship contests. Judges for the trials are brought in from Scotland and

New Zealand, where the competition ranks with soccer as national sporting events. The earliest known trials took place in Wales back in 1871.

Meeker area sheep ranchers make a special point to round up animals not familiar with dogs as herders. This is one feature which has made the contest a "must do" event for trainers in the United States and Canada. Another is the setting in a beautiful valley more than 6,000 feet above sea level.

To the applause of those in the stands, the dogs walk proudly off the field following their triumphs, and then may soak in a tub of water to relieve the heat and strain of their demanding task of quick running and tense alertness.

Recently, a bronze statue at the county courthouse in Meeker has been placed to celebrate and honor the canny canine competitors. It displays a dog crouching to intimidate three sheep.

76

A CHRISTMAS TREE IN THE DESERT
Who Decorates It?

The forty miles of highway between Grand Junction and Delta cross a desert region. Most of the road is quite straight with broad curves. About fifteen miles from Delta is what local people call "Fools' Hill." Probably the reason for that appellation is the sharp, steep "S" curve that has accounted for many automobile accident deaths, even though it has been improved several times. At the summit of the hill, near the highway, there was a lonely piñon pine tree, the only one for miles along the road.

The original piñon tree at the top of "Fool's Hill" between Delta and Grand Junction is gone but has been replaced. Author's Photo

A few decades ago, the tree mysteriously appeared with baubles and festoons at Christmas time. No one knew who or how many people might have been involved in the decoration.

It received national attention when television commentator Charles Kuralt included a segment on the tree in his "On the Road" broadcast. Later the pine died. Someone took the decorations a little too far, making it glow with lights powered by a battery. These dried out the old tree, which had struggled for life in a region where little more than seven inches of precipitation falls each year.

Laments over the demise of the tree moved the Highway Department to plant a new evergreen in its place. Every December the new tree, watered carefully, has been arrayed with colorful balls and bedecked with sparkling tinsel to carry on the tradition.

Many articles have been written about this custom, but no one seems to know for certain how it began. Was it a memorial to some loved one who died on Fools' Hill? Was it merely a fancy that something spectacular should appear on the desert scenery? Does anyone actually take responsibility, or is it just a general belief that the practice must continue?

Part Six

ORDEALS BY FIRE AND ICE

Mountains are continuously on the move. Sometimes landfalls alter the "best-laid plans of mice and men." Then there are winters which freeze the animals and sweep human beings to icy graves. Wildfires roar through the forests and grasslands. Mining is always dangerous, but explosions of coal dust are among the most disastrous events that can occur in any industrial pursuit.

77

LETHAL AVALANCHES IN THE SAN JUAN MOUNTAINS

Jack Bell's Survival "Never Eclipsed in Reality"

Snowslides, with their terrifying sudden death, have been recorded throughout the mountainous regions of Colorado. Many are the stories of disaster and sometimes miraculous survival. The San Juan Mountain Range has hundreds of slide slopes with common enough avalanches to have earned them names.

To the best of this writer's research, the avalanche which caused the most deaths at one time was the Liberty Bell Slide above Telluride, in 1907. It came roaring down on a mining boarding house one night, killing all seventeen men sleeping there. A party of six miners was recruited to bring out the bodies, but they, too, were killed when a second slide came down. Thus, this one terrible night accounted for twenty-three bodies.

Once an individual is caught and ploughed under by an avalanche, there is little chance of survival. The snow is packed around one like cement, and often there is no way of knowing which way is up. In modern times, at least one man in a closed car was rescued alive after eighteen hours, but even that was a very good stroke of luck. Before the automobile, travel in the winter over the mountain passes was usually by foot or on horseback, as the trails were so packed with snow that wagons could not be used.

Red Mountain Pass is located between Ouray and Silverton. Although kept open year around, it is considered a precarious journey even today, fraught with the danger of forty-one slide areas. Most notorious of these is the massive East Riverside slide which may claim its own record of deaths in recorded history.

In late February of 1897, Jack Bell was the mail carrier between Ouray and the mining camp of Ironton on that road. He led one horse, had another one packed with packages, and a companion led the way on still another horse. When the snow became very deep, Bell guided his horses although he had to cut his way through with a shovel. As he picked up the reins of his horse, the Riverside slide came roaring down on him. His partner, who was not caught in the full impact, saw nothing when he looked back, and realizing Bell was buried, set off for Ironton to seek a rescue crew. The journey took him two hours through deep snow.

From what Jack later remembered, he recovered consciousness and thought he was doomed. Then he felt the hard blade of his shovel on his face. It had created a small air space, which had kept him alive. After hours of struggle in the blackness, Bell managed to work his legs out of their imprisonment, and grasp his shovel. Not knowing whether he was digging the right direction, he began to work a little tunnel.

In the meantime, the rescue crew had arrived. They found the express package animal had drifted with the slide and was finally coaxed up to the trail. Bell's horse was also found dead beneath the snow with a broken neck. The mail pouch was also found, but after hours of prodding the slide with poles, all hope for rescue was abandoned, and word was sent to Jack's "widow" in Ouray. She collapsed when she got the word.

It was the next morning before the letter carrier worked himself to the daylight with his shovel. He had managed to make his way to the surface, but was so worn out and cold that he could only crawl his way past the toll gate at Bear Creek Falls, and feebly yell for help. It was fortunate Harry Lewis was on the way up and heard his call. Thus, a short time later, Jack was back in the arms of an overjoyed Mrs. Bell. He had been buried alive for more than twenty-four hours.

Ouray's newspaper, the *Herald*, commented: "Seldom in fiction, and certainly never in reality, has the experience been eclipsed." It may still be a record for such survival.

Heroic highway workers risk their lives frequently to keep the highways open in the winter. Several have been swept away to their deaths. Rescue workers have sometimes been aided in finding victims still alive with the use of very cleverly trained dogs.

Slides kill cross-country skiers almost every winter. One device which has been of help in recent times is an electronic beacon carried by the skier, by which he or she can be located, with luck, before death. No skier in avalanche country should leave home without one.

The Crested Butte coal disaster was national news in 1884. This illustration appeared in Harper's Weekly *on February 16, 1884. Courtesy of P. David Smith*

78

UNDERGROUND HOLOCAUSTS

Human Sacrifices to "King Coal"

Even today, with many safety precautions and regulations, an underground miner is subject to instant death from rockfalls, mechanical accidents, or even explosions. A century ago there were very few concerns over such matters as human safety. Coal miners still alive even in the twentieth century remember that the first question asked by mine operators following a disaster was how many mules were killed. Fed by a constant supply of immigrants, the human factor was secondary. Three of the greatest calamities in Western Slope history took place at Crested Butte, New Castle, and Mount Harris.

At the Jokerville Mine above Crested Butte, on January 24, 1884, a massive explosion of accumulated methane gas blew up near the entrance. The only fan which could ventilate the deeper chambers was put out of operation. Miners in the forward chambers were killed instantly; those further down were cut off from oxygen.

It was later learned that seventeen of the miners had groped their way to within 200 feet of the entrance when they fell from suffocation. Attempts to repair the ventilating fan came to naught. At least fifty-nine men were killed in that one disaster.

Another horrible blast shook the town of New Castle on February 18, 1896. Across the Colorado River, black smoke and poison gas issued from the Vulcan Mine, where some timbers had been thrown 400 feet into the river below. The explosion was at 11:27 A.M., but it was midnight before the first bodies were brought from 450 feet into the mine. Despite heroic rescue efforts, all forty-nine miners were killed. They were all Italian immigrants.

The Vulcan eventually resumed operation, and in 1913 excessive coal dust exploded, killing thirty-seven more men. Then the Vulcan was sealed forever, but one fire in it was never extinguished. Where it gets oxygen to continue is not known, but it still burns, forcing a tiny wisp of smoke through the mountain surface and showing spots where the winter snowcover has melted from the warmth of the smouldering coal below, nature's constant reminder of the calamities.

Thirty-four men were killed when the Wadge Mine in Routt County at Mount Harris blew up in a gas explosion. On January 27, 1942, the disaster occurred at 10:00 P.M.. Fellow miners rushed to the scene and risked their lives in a vain effort to find the victims, but there were only four survivors of that disaster a few miles east of the town of Hayden.

79

THE GREAT GUNNISON DIE-OFF

Deer Can't Digest Hay

W hen Western Colorado was first settled by miners and farmers, thousands of people depended on deer and elk as their main sources of food. By the beginning of the twentieth century, the herds had been so hunted down that it was a novelty to see either of these big game animals. A herd of elk was brought down from Wyoming to try to re-establish the wildlife balance. Between the years 1913 and 1917, no hunting licenses were issued.

Several factors led to the recovery of the animals. There was a bounty on their natural enemy, the mountain lion, until 1965 because the animal was a threat to cattle and sheep. Grizzly bears neared extinction. Careful regulation of hunting gradually restored the herds. By the 1930s there were almost too many deer for the available grazing land.

In the frigid winter of 1942 the wildlife service had to pick up the bodies of no less than 5,266 deer who had died slow, agonizing deaths from malnutrition due to overgrazing in the Gunnison area alone. It became known as the "Gunnison Die-off." While a large amount of money had been spent to spread hay to the starving animals, it was realized then that the hay impacted the intestines of the deer, and the practice was discontinued. Still, the hungry ruminants would attack the haystacks of ranchers and die nearby.

Winter in 1978-79 was the coldest Gunnison had experienced in fifty years. This time special pellets had been made for feeding the deer. People came from as far away as Grand Junction to help local volunteers get food to the emaciated animals. In spite of all these efforts, spring found thousands of bodies of deer along the fences; the animals were too weak to jump over. They just died on the spot.

There are those who are opposed to big game hunting, a major economic factor in Western Colorado. They might be equally alarmed to witness the pathetic sight of slowly starving animals. While disease and other natural factors sometimes control the population, there are probably more deer today than there were before the white man arrived. The hunter has become a necessary part of the balance of nature as humans have encroached upon primitive wildlife areas.

These antelope flee a grass fire probably started by the train, while "sportsmen" shoot at them from the train. Courtesy of P. David Smith Harper's Weekly, *May 29, 1875*

80

COLORADO'S LARGEST GRASSLAND CONFLAGRATION

The Infamous "I Do" Fire

On July 16, 1988 lightning touched off a grassland blaze southwest of the town of Maybell in Moffat County. Before it was contained, the flames had consumed more than 15,000 acres making it the largest prairie fire recorded in Colorado history.

Covering both private and public property, it did not consume buildings, and only a few isolated trees were burned. Antelope, deer and other small animals were driven through thick growths of grassland before the quick-spreading flames.

Volunteers from all over the region ran to try to stop the conflagration, which had a fire line of twenty-two miles in circumference. Word of the blaze reached a firefighter for the Bureau of Land Management at the moment when he was taking his wedding vows. He had to shout "I Do!" and rush immediately to the raging blaze, thus immortalizing the scorching flames as the "I Do" fire.

A point of interest sign along U.S. Highway 40, six miles from Maybell, explains that the region was replanted with wheat grass and rye in strips at right angles to the prevailing winds to reduce erosion until the range was eventually revegetated. Now those prairie lands furnish pasture for many thousands of big game animals and birds.

81

THE ROCKIES ON THE MOVE

Two Gigantic Landslides

Snowpacks and rainfalls in Western Colorado were heavy during the years of 1981 through 1985. In spite of two "hundred year floods" on the North Fork of the Gunnison River in 1983 and 1984, much of the moisture seeped deep into the mountain soils. In May of 1986 this underground water touched off the largest earthslide in United States history, except for that of the Mount St. Helens volcanic explosion.

This drift began on the lower reaches of Ragged Mountain, about twenty-one miles from Paonia above the Paonia Reservoir. The slippage was gradual, but the whole expanse of 140 million cubic yards, covering more than 1060 acres, started down the slope at about a foot per hour continuing until it had dammed Muddy Creek and flowed on over the existing Highway 133.

Crews worked twenty-four hour days to keep the stream open and prevent the buildup of a forty-foot dam and a new lake. Trees came floating down atop the mud. The scarp was that deep at the bottom but ranged from 100 to 150 feet in depth higher up. It swept everything on top along with it including the ranch home of Mrs. John Volk, a widow.

Now known as the McClure Pass Slide, because that was the route it closed, the flow continued through the early summer but slowed to only about ten feet a day by July.

At last highway workers could begin building a new highway some forty feet higher than the previous route. The breadth at the bottom of the slide was about 3,500 feet. Geologists came from great distances to view the slide that summer.

166

Some fissures from the slide can still be seen, and some trees, growing at odd angles, are yet visible from the highway.

Eons older, but far slower, is the famous Slumgullion Slide on the pass of that name between Lake City and Creede. A yellow mass of decomposed minerals in clay, this constantly creeping mass has probably been flowing down from the Continental Divide for countless ages. It created Lake San Cristobal beneath Cannibal Plateau, so named for Alferd Packer, who consumed the bodies of his partners there in 1874.

The region has had a long history of successful gold and silver mining. Geologist Dell Foutz has determined that there are many corroded forms of precious metals within the clay of the slide itself. Trees along Slumgullion Pass still "go with the flow" and grow at strange angles on the surface of that ancient slide.

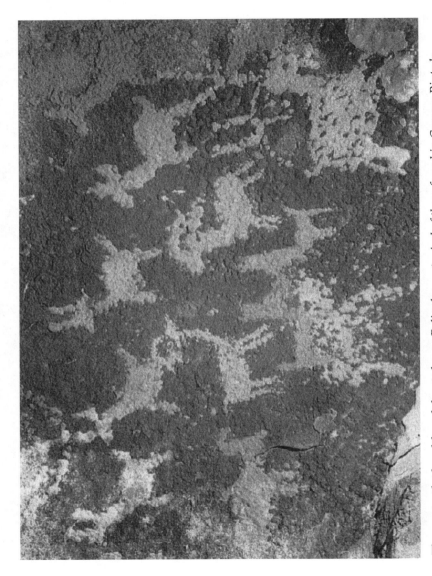

These petroglyphs, although located near Palisade, are typical of those found in Canyon Pintado. Courtesy Jim Du Bois

Part Seven

CIVILIZING THE SLOPE

From the prehistoric pictographs to the dozen or more professional murals in Delta County and the stunning trompe l'oeil in Cortez, graphic illustrations have expressed the tradition and imagination of Western Coloradans. Music has evolved from the local town bands to the symphonic strains which echo off the peaks above Breckenridge, Ouray, Vail and Aspen each summer. Noted sculptors from all over America go to Paonia's foundry to cast their bronze creations. Fine pottery, glassware and jewelry have been cultivated as exquisite arts. Poets from the mountains to the valleys have gained national acclaim.

The arts have evolved from beginnings in which the prime motive for the objects was simply survival.

82

THE CANYON PINTADO ART GALLERY

It's Fifteen Miles Long

There is a delightful comment made by natives of the town, "Rangely, Colorado, isn't at the end of the world, but some say that with binoculars you can see it from here." Located near the Utah border in Rio Blanco County, it is the center of a great oil field. Close by is Canyon Pintado which stretches fifteen miles along Colorado State Highway 139. The canyon is probably the most accessible display of rock art in this state, both petroglyphs of chiseled forms and pictograph paintings.

These designs were noted in 1776 by Father Escalante in his journal of the first systematic exploration of what is now Colorado. It was he and the leader, Father Dominquez, who named it, Spanish for "painted canyon." Along the rock wall which overlooks Douglas Creek, the Fremont culture of A. D. 600-1300 had etched most of the fifty illustrations. Later paintings were added by the Ute Indians.

One of the most striking aspects of the pictures has to be red paints which have kept their color after a millennium of wind, freezing, baking and moisture. Probably made from a mixture of berry juice and possibly hemotite, a powdery form of iron oxide, these colors are still bright.

Among the figures are humans in Fremont trapezoid style, mountain sheep, concentric circles such as those seen in some modern art, snake-like lines, and simple handprints. There is also Kokopelli, the humpbacked flute player of Anasazi mythology, a bringer of fortune — both good and bad.

The convenience of this viewing along a paved highway is well worth the drive. It must be pointed out, of course, that these

170

pictures, like those in the Louvre, are strictly "look but don't touch." Even a hand placed on these ancient illustrations may cause some deterioration.

Canyon Pintado Historic District is a property protected by the National Register of Historic Places.

Indian pictographs can be found all over Western Colorado. This one represents bighorn sheep. Courtesy of P. David Smith

83

COLD-SHOULDERING A TUBA

Why the Valves Failed

Many yarns have been told about the cold winters in the town of Gunnison, and most of them are true. Plastic trash containers fall to pieces at thirty below zero, and brass even changes shape. In a recollection by George Root, who once wrote of being a tuba player in the local band back in 1883, he was asked to play for a political rally; both he and the director noted that the tuba was out of tune.

It turned out the valves had frozen. Root was told to go to a nearby bakery to thaw out the instrument and return for a solo section. The musician took the tuba in and placed it beside a hot oven, getting it back in shape, then stood just inside the door of the bakery, yet when he ran out to play the solo segment, he found that the valves had frozen again and "wouldn't turn for love nor money."

84

AMERICA'S ORIGINAL COWBOY BAND

There Were No Cowboys In It

Silverton, the mining town situated at well over 9,000 feet in elevation, is located among steep mountains with no range on which to raise cattle. The growing season is too short to raise any agricultural crops except for a few hardy kitchen gardens. That is why it is indeed strange that it was there that the first nationally-recognized "cowboy band" was formed in 1885.

A number of towns had bands, but this one, formed in 1885, was decked out in ten gallon cowboy hats and other ranch regalia. Members called themselves the "Original Dodge City Band." Their music was so popular that they were soon invited to perform in other towns, both in Colorado and other western states.

By 1889 the band was so famous that they were invited to perform at the inauguration of President Benjamin Harrison in Washington, D.C. They also took part in the Colorado inaugurations of Governors Routt and Adams. There is also evidence that the band was also located in Ouray.

It may have been only coincidental, but a century later Silverton became the site of summer gatherings of some of the most talented brass players in the West. These latter-day instrumental stylists have also gained wide recognition as they perform concerts in Silverton and other Colorado towns.

85

WHEN DELTA HAD OPERAS

Kearns' Gilbert and Sullivan Productions

In the latter part of the nineteenth century and the early years of the twentieth, many Colorado towns had what they called opera houses. While real operas may have been performed in such places as Denver, Leadville and Central City, they were almost never seen in the other opera houses. Traveling companies might show up with plays such as "Uncle Tom's Cabin," "East Lynn," or "The Cowboy and the Lady." There were local musical presentations, graduation ceremonies, and later, silent movies. The opera house also served for public meetings as needed.

When the town of Delta had a population of only 836 souls, it, too, had an opera house. In 1897 Thomas Kearns moved there from New York City. He had been a star in Gilbert and Sullivan light opera but was diagnosed with a lung disease and advised to move to Colorado. Arriving in Denver he looked over advertising brochures from several places. He did not want to join the myriads of tuberculosis patients in Denver and Colorado Springs. His hands fell on a circular issued by the Delta County Board of Trade.

This publication emphasized the county's great cattle and fruit production, the relative prosperity, and the lack of crime. It added that the town of Delta had a new opera house named the Anna-Dora. A whimsical sort of man, Kearns decided to go and take a look at the area.

It must have been a shock for the urbane actor to behold this small, bleak village, but he realized that even with his limited funds, he could afford to take up residence. Soon his health was improving, and he decided to stay there. After the first year, though, he was a bit bored with the lack of cultural stimulation. Thomas invited several of his fellow actors from the East to visit him, and they were fascinated with a "real" western town complete with its watering troughs and hitching posts on the main street.

As his money began to run short, Kearns began performing. Members of the Wednesday Musical Club sold tickets for his programs in which he played the violin, sang, and gave dramatic readings.

Later, he went to look at the opera house. It had been built on the second floor of a hardware store. Ray Simpson and Frank Sanders had built it, naming it for their daughters, Anna and Dora. There was a stage, two dressing rooms, and oil lamp footlights. It was not much, but it had possibilities. He wrote his idea in letters to his performing friends, and they agreed to join him in a trial production of "The Mikado."

Kearns conducted auditions and found at least minimum talent locally for supporting roles and spent months in training a proper chorus. He sent to New York for fabric from which local volunteers made kimonos. Others worked on the sets. From the East came three of Kearns' friends to take the leading parts.

At last, "The Mikado" was presented, and it had to run for several performances to allow the whole community to attend. Substituting for a full-fledged orchestra was only a piano played by Miss Alice Croxton, a very talented Deltan. Before long children were singing, whistling, or humming the tunes of the comic opera on their way to school. The next year Thomas followed up with "H.M.S. Pinafore." He then produced his own mix of music, "A Colonial Extravaganza." This was followed by his "Broadway Revue."

Thomas Kearns had made the most of his remaining years. He died in 1903. No other operas were performed in Delta until the late 1980s when a local performing group, accompanied by the Valley Symphony Orchestra, began once more to produce some of the delightful musical classics.

86

SCHOLARS AND MUSICIANS AT GUNNISON
Western State's Impressive Summer Faculties

As the first higher education facility in Western Colorado, Gunnison's Colorado State Normal School, later to become Western State College, was expected to bring culture to the somewhat untamed region. With a cool and invigorating summer climate, the college attracted some truly famous scholars, writers, and musicians to spend the summer as guest faculty members.

Among the first of these was David Starr Jordan. Jordan was a biologist but had risen to the presidency of Indiana University. He then became the first chancellor of Stanford University. A personal friend of then President Woodrow Wilson, Jordan later would contribute to the "Fourteen Points" which brought an end to World War I. Jordan's lectures included topics from fish in the Black Canyon to world politics.

During the 1920s, guest faculty members included the two famous poets, Padraic Colum and Vachel Lindsay. Violinist Jules Falk also spent the summer as the college developed a symphony orchestra.

In the decades following World War II, Western started a summer music camp which became nationally famous. Composer in residence for a number of years was Ferde Grofe.

Grofe had orchestrated for Paul Whiteman Gershwin's "Rhapsody in Blue" but was even more famous for "Grand Canyon Suite." A man of considerable weight in his later years, the musician had to book two seats on the little Frontier Airlines planes which carried him to and from Gunnison. During his years there, he composed "Valley of Enchantment" inspired by the Cochetopa pasturelands nearby and "Black Canyon Suite."

Another regular member of the summer faculty was William Revelli, director of the Michigan University bands, often regarded as among the finest in America.

A full-time faculty member during the prewar years had been Alan Swallow who wrote popular novels and non-fiction. He later founded Sage Books and the Swallow Press, major publishers in Colorado.

The Original Cowboy Band was hired out to the Ouray Elk's Club in this photo taken in Salt Lake City. Courtesy of P. David Smith

87

THE PERRY-MANSFIELD DANCING CAMP

Cheesecloth Costumes at Strawberry Park

Charlotte Perry and Portia Mansfield were the creators of one of the first art and culture centers in Western Colorado. Both had been educated at Smith College, and both had become enthralled by interpretive and classical forms of dance. Miss Perry's family owned a coal mine at Oak Creek, and in vacationing there, she discovered Steamboat Springs and its nearby beautiful Strawberry Park.

Just after World War I the two decided that there should be a hideaway for the daughters of prosperous families to partake in the dance styles which were being re-discovered and enlarged upon by the avant-garde tastes of the cultural elite.

There, overlooking the valley below, they established the Perry-Mansfield Dancing Camp. It was secluded enough that the girls who took part could be protected from the harsh realities of a rough cowboy town and the disapproving eyes of those who frowned upon dancing in general, much less Greco-Roman forms. The school admitted girls from affluent backgrounds, ages twelve to twenty-five.

It was truly a camp, with the ladies living in tents, although there was a wood-constructed, rustic-style dining hall with mosquito netting to add to the comforts. The girls took part in interpretive dances on the grasslands and among the trees, clad in costumes made of cheesecloth.

The participants were not totally restricted to the camp and were permitted to shop in town, much to the gratification of local merchants. Before long the camp had established a national reputation, and its opening each June was a major event in Steamboat Springs. Residents would go to meet the train which carried the students from Denver and were there to see them off at the end of the season.

As it grew the school introduced music instruction and dramatics, as well as horseback riding, to its curriculum, and added some historical instruction. Julie Harris was one of the famous actresses who had been an apprentice at the camp. More attractive housing was later added. A theater, named for Harris, was built in the 1960s.

The founders eventually turned the operation of the camp over to prestigious Stevens College of Columbia, Missouri, which brought the promise of permanence to the venture.

Women of not so good a character dance for men in Denver
P. David Smith Collection

88

WHEN BROADWAY CAME TO GRAND JUNCTION

Glory Days at the Avalon

Time was when nationally-famous entertainers who took their shows on the road needed two days for the rail journey from Denver to Salt Lake City in order to stay refreshed. Thus, in the 1920s and '30s, Grand Junction was often an overnight stop. In order to justify the expense, many of them would make a performance there.

This led to the construction of the large Avalon Theater on the main street of Grand Junction. Magicians, singers and dramatists performed shows throughout the years. Among the famous names who appeared were: Al Jolson, Rudy Vallee, the Ink Spots, Tony Sarg's Marionette Show and the popular radio attraction, Rubinoff and his Violin. As the "picture shows" gained sound, the Avalon was sold for a movie theater and was redecorated in the art deco fashion so popular in the '30s.

After World War II a number of Broadway shows began to go on nationwide tours, and some of them were performed in Grand Junction, but they had to settle for the Mesa College gymnasium-cum-theater or later, the larger Grand Junction High School auditorium.

The productions included such musicals as Leonard Bernstein's "Candide," as well as "Kismet" and "The Unsinkable Molly Brown." The Scopes trial drama, "Inherit the Wind" was also performed there.

When the traveling cast of Archibald MacLeish's "J.B." was presented in the new high school auditorium star John Carradine announced that the sets were snowbound on Loveland Pass. The cast decided the show could still go on. Using ladders and benches on a bare stage, the performance of the actors was dynamic, a unique experience for a Western Slope audience.

The Avalon has been restored to its original tasteful setting and attracts varied touring groups as well as locally-produced shows today.

Many a performer got off the train at the Grand Junction depot in the 1920s and '30s. Courtesy of P. David Smith

181

89

GRAND JUNCTION'S PROBLEM WITH DALTON TRUMBO

"Shale City" Never Forgave the Famous Writer

Dalton Trumbo was one of the most renowned of Hollywood screenwriters and a novelist of note. He was born in Montrose but grew up in Grand Junction, where his father worked for a local retailer. Trumbo himself became a reporter for the Grand Junction *Daily Sentinel* and it was the publisher of that newspaper who helped the youth get into the University of Colorado. When Trumbo's father was fired, the embittered writer dropped out and moved to Los Angeles.

It was there that he wrote his first novel, *Eclipse*. Set in the town of "Shale City, Colorado," it had as its protagonist one John Abbott who was quickly identified as William Moyer, one of Grand Junction's most honored citizens, and there were other characterizations of local denizens, both favorable and unfavorable. The novel did cast some aspersions on the general population and recognized the existence of prostitution. When Trumbo tried to market it, American publishers found the book too hot to handle, but it was published in London, England, in 1935.

There never was a second edition. It is probable that the plates were destroyed in the bombing of London during World War II, but a local account claims that a Grand Junction man bought the plates and destroyed them. There is no doubt that the novel was purchased and read but then probably destroyed by many Grand Junctionites. *Eclipse* is now much in demand on the rare book market commanding a high price.

182

Shale City was the setting for several other works by Trumbo. His play, "The Biggest Thief in Town," is a hilarious spoof of the local newspaper and a mortician. It had its opening in London and was a hit until the lead actor died. This play has amused audiences of local theater groups in Gunnison and Montrose, but as of this writing it has not appeared on any Grand Junction stage.

The "mythical town" also appeared in his *Magnificent Andrew,* and briefly in his shocking war story, *Johnny Got His Gun.* Trumbo was a dedicated pacifist. When he was asked to testify against fellow actors during the McCarthy era, he refused and was placed on the notorious "Hollywood Black List." Writing with a nom-de-plume of Robert Rich, he won an Academy Award in 1956 for his movie, "The Brave One." It was not until 1975, after exoneration as a possible Communist, that he received the award in his own name.

Among the most famous of his scripts were "Exodus," "Spartacus" and "Thirty Seconds Over Tokyo." There were many more works, but whenever they played at Grand Junction movie theaters, the home-town boy's name was never mentioned on the marquees.

90

THE ERUDITE AND MUSICAL INVASION OF ASPEN

Celebrating the Goethe Bicentennial

Aspen was still a rather shabby former mining town in the summer of 1949 when probably the largest gathering of prominent intellectuals and musicians in Western Colorado took place. It was a celebration of the bicentennial of the birth of Johann Wolfgang Von Goethe, one of the world's most famous German poets and the originator of the "Sturm und Drang" literary movement.

Industrialist Walter Paepcke, who developed Aspen as a ski area three years earlier, was also a great fan of Goethe, and could recite passages of the play, "Faust." He was also a close associate of Chancellor Robert Hutchins of the University of Chicago and philosopher Mortimer Adler.

At that time the world's most famous living philosopher was Nobelist Albert Schweitzer. His "reverence for life" concept had made him an international figure, but he was also one of the greatest interpreters of Bach's music, a master of the organ, and a dedicated physician. He had established the hospital colony of Lambarene in Africa where he devoted the rest of his life to the care of impoverished natives. At the age of seventy-four, he had never been to the United States until invited to give the keynote address at this tiny spot in the Colorado Rockies.

Another philosopher who left his beloved Spain for the first time to take part in that event, was Ortega y Gasset, most noted for his significant work, *Revolt of the Masses*. Thornton Wilder, Pulitzer Prize winner for his novel, *The Bridge of San Luis Rey* and again for his play, "Our Town," also arrived for the celebration.

Dmitiri Metropoulos and the Minneapolis Symphony Orchestra provided music with famed pianist Arthur Rubinstein. Opera star Dorothy Maynor was joined by Erica Morini and Nathan Milstein.

This event drew thousands of people and worldwide publicity. Adler explained that Aspen was thereafter to symbolize the Athenian ideal of arete, the perfect mind in a perfect body. All of this led to the establishment of The Aspen Institute for Humanistic Studies.

The Bicentennial also had an influence on summer activities in other Western Colorado towns. Breckenridge developed a noted musical institute; Ouray, Telluride, Winter Park, Silverton and Crested Butte eventually added musical and cultural attractions.

91

WESTERN COLORADO'S LARGEST ART CREATION

Twenty-Eight Months to Build; Twenty-Eight Hours to Collapse

On August 10, 1972 a huge curtain of bright orange hung across Rifle Gap, twelve miles north of the town of Rifle. It was the brain child of Christo and his wife, Jeanne-Claude, internationally famous as what they called "earth artists."

The first drawings of the 142,000 square feet of nylon fabric were done by Christo in March of 1970. The artists labored with donations of over half a million dollars and the volunteer help of sixty-four art students to get the curtain up by 1971, but the wind took it down in minutes. Undaunted, the Bulgarian-born Christo and his Parisian wife re-engineered the huge project.

The undertaking was scorned by some but admired by many who had an appreciation of the artists. Christo's first project had been the placement of 200 oil drums of various colors to block a narrow street in Paris. Since the Rifle Gap curtain, he has wrapped the Reichstag in Berlin, planted thousands of colorful umbrellas on a Japanese landscape, and created other astounding creations.

Total width of the curtain itself was 1,250 feet, hanging from a cable which spanned the canyon for 1,368 feet and weighed 110,000 pounds. Alas, only twenty-eight hours later, a sixty-miles-per-hour wind tore it and required removal of the project.

It had taken a full twenty-eight months to realize the dream from drawing board to reality. Christo, who does not use his last name of Janacheff, had studied art in his home country as well as in Czechoslovakia, Switzerland and France. He and his wife do not seek taxpayer funds for their projects but are able to market the paintings and photographs on a worldwide scale and also receive money from museum exhibitions of their work.

As of this writing, the sixty-four year old Christo has announced plans to cover a section of the Arkansas River near Salida which have encountered opposition.

Christo's "Valley Curtain 1970-72" at Grand Hogback in Rifle, Colorado

The Wild Bunch 1901. From left: The Sundance Kid, Will Carver, Ben Kilpatrick, Harvey Logan, and Butch Cassidy

Part Eight

SHAM DUELS AND OUTRAGEOUS OUTLAWS

This might be called saving the worst for last. There have been many books and stories about outlaws in Western Colorado, and there were plenty of them to write about. Few of the alleged face-offs actually turned out badly.

Doc Holliday and Kid Curry rot in Glenwood cemeteries. Harry Tracy escaped from both the Hahn's Peak and Aspen jails. Banks were robbed at Telluride, Delta and Meeker. Cattle rustlers, including the Stockton gang, ran rampant over the southwest. Butch Cassidy and the Wild Bunch holed up at Brown's Park along with Isom Dart, Matt Warner, and others. Trains were robbed at Whitewater and Parachute.

Here are a few incidents which are included because each had a unique aspect, not usual in outlaw stories. At least one is ghastly.

92

LAKE CITY'S FIRST DUEL

The Despair of "Doc" Kaye

It was September of 1877, and the mining town of Lake City was still in construction. It seems that a man known only as "The Taylor" had been insulted by a ruffian known as "Doc" Kaye, and the challenged party chose shotguns as weapons.

The ground was covered with an early snowfall. Seconds were chosen for the "affair of honor." They inspected the weapons and loaded them. Rules of the formal duel were fully explained.

"Doc" had fortified himself with several shots of whiskey and was "bellicose and courageous as Goliath of Gath." Taylor, on the other hand, appeared calm and very dignified.

The opponents stepped off the proper distance, and on the count of three, two-shotgun blasts echoed up and down the canyon walls. "Doc" fired point blank, but Taylor shot wild, grasped his chest, and fell to the ground, issuing what appeared to be life blood on the snowy ground.

The "doctor" stood in horror of what he had done. Then he ran to a nearby excavation and threw himself into it, burying his head in the water. When he was pulled out, to his amazement it was by "The Taylor!"

It seems everyone but "Doc" knew the weapons were loaded with blanks, and the blood was simply a sponge full of red ink. The two men apologized to each other and became fast friends.

93

ANOTHER SURPRISING DUEL

The Great Powderhorn Showdown

The settlement known as Powderhorn may be found between Gunnison and Lake City. It was the site of considerable mining and ranching activity between 1880 and 1882. That was when a young man named John Cogan came to the valley and began working for John R. Smith.

Smith told Cogan, whose intelligence, according to one observer, was "decidedly inferior," that Cogan ought to get married and mentioned an eligible young lady. Cogan, before he had even met this young lady, began to tell people he was going to marry her.

Smith, thinking he was a practical joker, told Cogan that he would stand behind him, reporting that Andy Stone, who was courting the young lady, was jealous and was saying Cogan had insulted her. Smith then convinced Cogan that a duel was in order and that Stone was a coward who would refuse to shoot, thus making Cogan a local hero.

Smith took Cogan to the justice of the peace to write a challenge. It was delivered to Stone, who accepted with reluctance.

Everyone assembled at a local bridge where the affair of honor was to take place. Pistols were placed three feet in front of each of the men who stood at opposite ends of the bridge. At the signal each man grabbed his weapon to begin firing. Andy stood firm and pretended to be taking careful aim. Cogan fired into the bridge near Stone and began to advance, crying "I have you now!" Then his pistol misfired.

John Cogan came up with a new idea. He told Stone that if Stone would give him five hundred dollars, he would withdraw the challenge. Stone replied that he was not rich enough to pay that amount. Gradually Cogan kept reducing the amount asked. When he reached zero, Stone still would not call off the duel.

At last, Cogan offered Stone twenty-five dollars to cancel the deal. By this time Stone claimed that honor was honor, and the shooting must resume. Reloading weapons, each man was ready to fire. Cogan took another shot, realized he was a very poor marksman, and began to run. Pursued by Stone, Cogan threw a rock which knocked down the opponent, ending the confrontation.

When John Cogan found out that he had been set up, he did not appreciate Smith's machinations at all and left the valley in embarrassment.

94

THAT SLOPPY HANGING IN LAKE CITY

There Was No Boy Scout Manual to Instruct the Mob

While impromptu hangings loom large in the lore of the Old West, it seems that many who participated in such lynchings did not know how to tie a proper hangman's noose. Properly formed, this knot will break the neck of the victim causing instant death.

There were probably hundreds of men who slowly strangled as a result of amateurs who undertook the execution process. One example of poor knot-tying took place April 26, 1882, in Lake City, Colorado.

It seems that two nefarious characters, George Betts and James Browning, owned a saloon of dubious repute in that mining camp. Browning was but a youth of eighteen years. They had taken to entertaining two dance-hall girls in the vacant home of W.G. Luckett, who was not in town at the time. On their first visit the trespassers were so intrigued with the fine furnishings and antiques in the home that they stole some of the articles which were later found to be in their possession.

This foursome was quite pleased with their loot and planned another visit to steal some more articles on April 25. However Luckett had returned to town and found his home had been burglarized. He called on the popular sheriff, E. N. Campbell, who with his deputy, Clair Smith, went to the house to investigate that afternoon. While they were in a dark hall, the culprits entered and lit matches which clearly identified themselves.

Ordered to drop their firearms, Betts instead shot Campbell, who made an attempt to return fire before dropping dead. Smith tried to revive the stricken sheriff while the two criminals escaped.

Betts was soon captured trying to get away on the Slumgullion Pass road; young Browning was caught hiding in the saloon. A coroner's jury met and found that the bullet which killed Campbell matched Betts's pistol. Betts was charged with murder, Browning as accessory. Both men were confined in the local jail.

That night a large crowd of outraged citizens decided to act on their own rather than go through the expense and anguish of a trial. By 11:00 P.M., the crown was masked and armed with sledge hammers and ropes. Some reports claimed that every able-bodied man in town was in the mob.

The guards at the jail ordered the attackers to stop, but soon lowered their own rifles and joined in the lynching. The two culprits were dragged from the jail to the Ocean Wave bridge, just north of the town. There, in the early morning hours of April 26, they were hanged.

Perhaps there was a decent job done on the noose for Betts, but poor Browning made many futile attempts with his manacled hands to seize the rope from which he was suspended. It took him a long time to die.

Pronouncing the men "hanged by unknown parties," the coroner closed the case. School was dismissed so that the children could view the bodies still hanging. This was considered an important object lesson in proper citizenship.

The two girls who had been in on the original theft disappeared from town. The community confiscated the saloon and later sold it as a dance hall, and then passed an ordinance which prohibited prostitutes from entering saloons or soliciting on the streets at night.

As for the Ocean Wave bridge, it was a tourist attraction for several decades.

95

THE TRAGEDY AT GRAND LAKE

Demise of Five County Officials

Several counties have changed the seat of their governments. Hahn's Peak was the site of the courthouse for Routt County until the railroad came to Steamboat Springs. When mining wealth declined at Rico, Dove Creek became the Dolores County seat, although some stories claim that there was a raid in which the records were stolen and taken to the then more prosperous bean-growing town. When Grand Lake, with a booming mining economy, attempted to move the center of politics from Hot Sulphur Springs in Grand County, bloodshed of an unprecedented magnitude in American history for such a cause was the tragic result. A brief summary of the activities there neglects the animosity which had been growing for several years, prior to the shootings on July 4, 1883.

County Commissioners Barney Day and Edward P. Weber, supporters of moving the county seat to Grand Lake, had just breakfasted with County Clerk Thomas J. Dean. As the three left the hotel beside the lake, they were ambushed by four masked men. It was expected by the attackers that the fireworks that morning would disguise the sound of real bullets being fired.

Those who perpetrated the onslaught were John Mills, himself a Commissioner, Sheriff Charles Royer, and Undersheriff William Redman, along with his brother, Mann. They were determined to put an end to the bitter political struggle which had seen election ballots favor one town, claims of ballot stuffing, and corruption by officers.

All three of the officials were killed or died of wounds in the attack, but one fired back, killing one of the masked men. The other three escaped. When the body of the attacker was unmasked, the shock was unbelievable. It was Mills, the third Commissioner.

The sheriff and undersheriff had quickly returned to Hot Sulphur Springs. They were then sent for to investigate the crime they had committed themselves! There was no immediate explanation forthcoming. No posse was formed; no evidence of concern was shown by Royer.

A few days later, Sheriff Royer went to Georgetown. He took a room in the hotel there and proceeded to shoot himself in the head. The suicide was the fifth victim of the horrible affair.

Redman disappeared shortly after that. Some weeks later, near the Utah border, a body was found shot to death. Nearby was a saddle with the name of Redman on it, and the name had also been marked in the sand at the site. Whether he had killed himself or had been murdered was never determined. No one there could identify the body as being that of Redman. He may have been the sixth victim.

The county seat is still at Hot Sulphur Springs, but the horrible events of 1883 will never be forgotten.

Yachting has always been a favorite summer sport at Grand Lake. Courtesy of P. David Smith

96

QUEEN OF THE CATTLE RUSTLERS

Ann Basset of Brown's Park

If any one area of Colorado could be so designated, Brown's Hole, or Park, as it was known, in the extreme northwest corner of the state, had the greatest concentration of outlaws. The list of miscreants reads like a rogues' gallery: Butch Cassidy, Harvey Logan, Harry Longsbaugh, Bill and Tom McCarty, Harry Tracy, Tom Horn, Bob Meldrum, Matt Warner, Isom Dart, and others. John Rolfe Burroughs has recorded the details of that region in his excellent book, *Where the Old West Stayed Young.*

Central to the valley was the Basset Ranch. Ann Basset, born in 1878, was the first white child born in northwestern Colorado. With her younger sister and brother, she had a proper upbringing under the guidance of a gentle mother and respected father. Her parents soon realized that she was something of a maverick. She went to school in Craig, but upon returning spent more time at the bunk house reading copies of the *Police Gazette*, learning to swear, and breaking wild horses. Sent to a private school in Salt Lake City, she then went to a good Boston finishing school. It was there that she learned proper Victorian behavior, although on probation most of the time.

In due course, she returned to the ranch and still persisted in raucous methods, although as Burroughs described it, she had a "Dr. Jekyll and Mr. Hyde" personality. Her main antagonism in life was against the wealthy absentee ranch barons who often exploited the small cattlemen.

Ann married a respected ranchman, Hi Bernard, but his efforts to control her whims eventually overwhelmed him. She was as congenial to some of the most reprehensible of the outlaws as to some of the most honorable ranchers. She could impress the other women with her refined manners and careful apparel, but she could also swear like a trooper.

While Hi was away at Denver one time, Ann invited another cowpuncher and another ranchwoman to move in with her. Upon his return, Hi decided to build a teepee for himself rather than to join the crowd. As he listened to the laughter and songs coming from his house, Hi decided that he'd had enough and divorced her.

Ann's most hated enemy was multimillionaire Ora Haley who owned a nearby ranch with many thousands of cattle. It was true, as she later wrote, that she and her new boyfriend felt free to rustle cattle for their table from that huge business. When Haley hired a spy they were nabbed and charged. The first trial in Craig had to be held in the opera house to contain all of the crowd who sympathized with Ann. It ended in a hung jury. Her partner later skipped town, and Ann Basset had to be re-tried alone. She was acquitted of the charges, and Craig citizens staged a parade, complete with band, in celebration. Most of the citizenry of what was then Routt County detested the cattle kings. In court Ann deported herself with such refined class that nobody could really believe she was anything but a lady who would not engage in illegal activities.

Ann married again, and she and her husband homesteaded a ranch in Arizona. They later moved to Utah, where she died in 1956 at the age of seventy-eight.

97

"NOT MUCH DAMAGE DONE"

Trial of a Harvey Gap Murderer

Horace Greeley Brown settled on a ranch near the town of Rifle in 1883. It was not long before he became a deputy sheriff in Garfield County. He later told of shooting a murderer who had apparently been well-liked.

Brown must have had other disagreeable duties. He remembered that several attempts were made on his life. At one time carbolic acid was put in his cough syrup. Later he was told that a man was going to hang him and replied "If you do, I'll find out and I won't like it a bit."

Another story he remembered was that of a shooting at a saloon where the Harvey Gap Reservoir was under construction. Almost every man carried a revolver in those days, and it seems that one James Pilgrim, known as "Jamie," had killed another man before several witnesses. Both men had been drinking.

Brown was called upon to arrest the murderer and take him to Glenwood Springs to be tried. Binding Jamie's hands and leading his horse, Brown ran into a crowd of rowdies as they passed through the town of New Castle. They did not seem to know either the victim or the killer, but were intent on the idea of a lynching just for the excitement of it all. Brown was able to threaten them adequately to proceed to Glenwood where Jamie was incarcerated.

The next morning a six-man jury was seated, and the accused man, as was the custom at that time, stood before the court. He was poised and apparently not afraid, facing whatever fate might await him. Several witnesses testified. Did the victim seem to be attacking? No, it was not in any case a matter of self-defense. Had the victim cheated at cards? No, there was no card game. What was the person-ality of the murdered man? On this point, none who knew him could say anything good. He was simply a crude character given to foul comments in his work and in the saloon.

Interrogated, Jamie admitted the shooting. He did not plead any cause except that the victim talked abusively and was known as a bully. The jury then met, and as Pilgrim faced the court, a decision was reached.

In what must be unique in Western Colorado jurisdiction, the verdict was: "Found guilty of killing, but not much damage done, so we desire he be given his freedom." Jamie returned to his work on Harvey Gap Reservoir the next day, according to the Brown's story.

98

RAY SIMPSON'S REMARKABLE MARKSMANSHIP

Shooting the McCartys out of their Saddles

One of the most notorious outlaw bands in the West was that of Tom and Bill McCarty who were perpetrators of several bank robberies. At various times their cohorts included Butch Cassidy and Matt Warner. In Colorado they robbed banks in Denver and Telluride.

Their last holdup was on September 7, 1893 in Delta. Tom and Bill, and Bill's son, teenager Fred, robbed the Farmers and Merchants Bank. Tom held three horses in the alley behind the bank while Bill and Fred entered and demanded money at gunpoint from Trew Blachly, manager, and his assistant, H. H. Wolbert. Blachly yelled out in alarm. Wolbert tried to reach for a pistol but was quickly covered. When Blachly cried out again, the impetuous Fred shot him dead.

Grabbing what they could, the two ran out the rear door and jumped on the horses running at full gallop.

Next door to the bank, Ray Simpson, a hardware dealer, was cleaning his Sharps single-shot rife. When he heard Blachly call out, Ray ran to the corner and took quick aim. He shot Bill through the head. Then he reloaded and killed Fred, still riding away, with a second shot. Tom was too far ahead to be picked off.

The reason for repeating this oft-told story is that most accounts of it attribute the quick shooting by Simpson to a repeating rifle. It was not. Sharps never made a repeating rifle. Simpson had to stop and re-load in what must have been record time in order to get off the second accurate shot. The rifle is on display in the Delta historical museum. This must have been one of the most remarkable shooting feats in the entire lore of western gunfighting.

As for Tom McCarty, there are so many accounts of what happened to him that nothing may be ascertained with validity. He did write threatening letters to Simpson later. He was supposedly seen in Montana, Utah, and Oregon and was reported killed, or as so many outlaws seem to do, lived to a ripe old age, according to the imagination of those who dote on such matters.

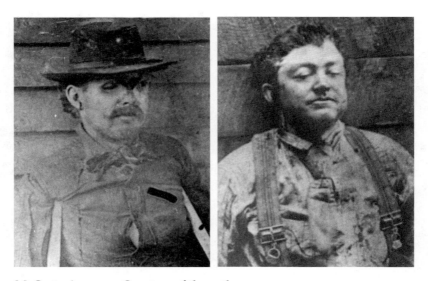

McCartys' corpses. Courtesy of the author.

99

A BEHEADING NEAR BEDROCK

And a Marketable Skull from Brown's Park

Probably the two most lawless places in Western Colorado were Brown's Park in Moffat County and the Paradox Valley in Montrose County. Both bordered on Utah and were far removed from legal authority; both were also prime routes for cattle rustling.

One gang of outlaws had a hangout near the town of Bedrock on the Dolores River in the Paradox Valley. It was said that they would remove the heads of their shooting victims in order to prevent identification. Two of the criminals, Dean Meyers and John Miller, decided to go after the money belt of Lemuel (Slim) Hecox.

Hecox, who claimed his real name was Hickock, said he was related to the infamous "Wild Bill" of that same appellation. Slim would brag that he carried his wealth strapped to his waist and would always be able to protect it with the pair of revolvers he toted. Some people believed the money was attained in a bank robbery some years before in Kansas.

It was in 1920 that Hecox was employed as a watchman in the Cashin Mine near Bedrock. The plan was that Meyers would go to visit with him some night, and when it was convenient, Miller would shoot Hecox from outside a window. The plan worked well. Slim thought the visitor was a friend, and only one shot was needed to kill the watchman.

They cut Slim's head off and then buried the body underneath bags of oats stored for the mules in a back room. One of the bags apparently broke open. The murderers then took the head some miles away and left it in an irrigation ditch.

When no one had seen Hecox for several weeks, some men went up to the mine. There they found blood on the floor and traced it back to the oat room. The headless corpse was found. By that time some of the oats had fallen into the stump of the neck and sprouted, making a horrifying sight.

Detectives were sent to the valley by the absentee owner of the mine, and they were able to determine the identity of the culprits and arrest them. Tried in Montrose, Meyers and Miller finally confessed and were sentenced to terms in the state penitentiary. They also told where they had left the head of the victim.

The head was recovered, and the coffin was dug up. As the coffin-maker did not want to waste lumber, he had made the box only long enough for Slim's torso and legs. His head was then placed in his left arm, and the whole body was once again interred.

Two decades before this incident, up in Brown's Park, William Pidgeon had been killed by Ike Lee. Before Lee later surrendered, he was camping when some friends came upon him. Lee kept stirring the pot of stew he had boiling, and his friends asked if they could sample it. They were startled to see Pidgeon's head in the pot.

It turned out that Lee had a friend whose clients included a doctor in Kansas City, Missouri. The doctor had needed a human skull, and Lee hoped to make a bit of money by providing a marketable specimen.

100

THOSE GRISLY SOAP-KETTLE MURDERS

A Horrifying Result of Child Abuse

While there are many conflicting facts that emerged in the investigation and trial, the most logical account of what happened is included here.

In December of 1917, John Bush and his son, Otis, were living with John's mother, Nancy, on California Mesa near the town of Olathe. It seems that Nancy had accused her grandson of stealing $1.35 from her pocketbook. John undertook to punish the twelve-year-old, and Nancy was aghast at the wails of the child in the back yard. Shortly thereafter John came into the house and reported that he had hurt the child badly.

He ordered his mother to get some lye which she used for making soap, and because she feared her son, she obeyed. In the meantime, John chopped up the body of his dead son and placed the parts in a huge kettle designed to make the soap. He then lit a fire beneath the kettle and boiled up the remains. After that, he burned the remaining bones and the boy's clothing in the kitchen stove.

How he could sleep after that, it is hard to imagine, but that is what Nancy later testified. She was worried that John would kill her as the only eyewitness to the murder. She maintained that she had only acted at gunpoint in her accessory actions.

While John slept, Nancy slipped into his room and killed him with an axe. Then she proceeded to chop him up.

Not as careful as her son had been, Nancy did not get rid of all the bones after she had also cooked up his remains. This and certain other evidence were presented to prove the murder charges against her.

There is some question as to what became of Nancy. Either she was sentenced to prison or declared insane and sent to the state asylum. It remains one of the most macabre stories of Montrose County.

Soap Kettle from 1895 Montgomery Ward Catalog

101

A GANGSTER RESORT AT SWEETWATER LAKE

Scarface Al Capone Was an Honored Guest

Hhis name was Leland Varain, but his most popular alias was Diamond Jack Alterie. He married Ermina Rossi, daughter of an alleged Colorado bootlegger. This was in the era of prohibition, and Diamond Jack was one of the most notorious gang leaders in Chicago. Even though it was known that he was a kingpin in the liquor business, he had his cover as Secretary of the Janitors' and Window Washers' Union.

When Jack was likely to be caught in a shady deal by the federal agents, or when a rival gang had fingered him, he took refuge at his elaborate resort on Sweetwater Lake.

Sweetwater Lake is about seventeen miles northwest of the village of Dotsero, not far from what is now the Flat Tops Wilderness Area. He had purchased a cabin on the lakeshore and procured a ten-year lease from the White River National Forest Service. He also seemed to have gained fishing rights to the shorefront. When fishing boats would come close to his territory, they were run off with tommy guns.

He built a luxurious hangout overlooking the lake, and had a resident staff. Diamond Jack was remarkably well-received for a time. He sported gaudy western wear, and gave fine gifts to lawmen and game wardens. Jack presented all the children at the Sweetwater School with Christmas presents of considerable value.

He invited a number of prominent friends out to Colorado to partake of fishing. Among them were the infamous "Legs" Diamond and "Scarface" Al Capone. At one time when Capone went to Glenwood Springs, staying at the Hotel Colorado, he visited a local jeweler to secure a platinum mounting for his six carat diamond. It seems the jeweler also sold phonograph records. When Capone could not decide which records he wanted to buy, he ordered his chauffeur to purchase the entire stock. It was believed that Capone may have had a fortune of some thirty million dollars before he was finally arrested for income tax evasion.

Gang warfare, including the "St. Valentine's Day Massacre," tore through Chicago in the late twenties, but the instigators were always missing; perhaps they were enjoying the hospitality of Diamond Jack. When prohibition ended, hard times befell their rackets. Dodging federal charges himself, Jack became less of a good guy.

When the popular pioneer, Carl Schleischer, went fishing on the lake, hoodlums shot his boat full of holes, and when he made his way to shore, he was pistol-whipped. This infuriated the citizenry of Garfield County. Alterie was arrested for having given the orders to get rid of Schleischer. The jury had to be recruited from the west end of Garfield County because anyone from the eastern region, where the lake is located, would be biased against Jack.

The Hotel Colorado in Glenwood Springs has always been a popular resort. Courtesy of P. David Smith

Charged with attempted murder and carrying concealed weapons, he pleaded guilty. Given the choice of a prison term or a fine of $1250 and orders to leave Colorado, the gangster chose the second course. It is said that he wept when he left his lovely hideout. He was dodging the income tax people himself but was fatally gunned down in Chicago by rivals soon after his return.

ACKNOWLEDGMENTS

The writer wishes to acknowledge the services provided by the staffs of the following museums, libraries and agencies:

Anasazi Heritage Museum, Dolores
Chevron Headquarters, Rangely
Cortez Public Library
Cozens Ranch Museum, Fraser
Craig-Moffat County, Library
Delta County Historical Museum
Delta Public Library
Grand County Museum, Hot Sulphur Springs
Hotchkiss-Crawford Museum, Hotchkiss
Mancos Museum
Meeker Historical Museum
Montrose Historical Museum
Montrose Public Library
Museum of Western Colorado, Grand Junction
North Fork Museum, Paonia
Northwest Colorado Museum, Craig
Ouray-Uinta Ute Reservation Headquarters, Fort Duschene, Utah
Paonia Public Library
Rangely Museum
Reed Library, Fort Lewis College
Rifle Public Library
Savage Library, Western State College
Southern Ute Museum, Ignacio
Tomlinson Library, Mesa State College
Tread of the Pioneers Museum, Steamboat Springs
Ute Indian Museum, Montrose
Western Colorado Center for the Arts, Grand Junction

and the following individuals who helped in many ways to make this book possible:

Jean Bader, Mancos
Jim DuBois, Grand Junction
Diana Fay, Granby
Joan Fay, Grand Junction
Marisa Fay, Palisade
Dell R. Foutz, Grand Junction
Tony Garcia, Jr., Delta
Thelma Kathrein, Grand Junction
Jan Koppri, Mancos
Bill Lemoine, Hotchkiss
Ken Reyher, Olathe
Dave Shafer, Fort Lewis
Betty Spehar, Crested Butte
Ron Steele, Bedrock
Louise Waid, Grand Junction
David and Oneta Wooten, Maybell
Ruby Wooten, Craig

BIBLIOGRAPHY

All places of publication are in Colorado unless otherwise noted.

Alsop, Kenneth. **The Bootleggers and Their Era**. Chicago, Ill. 1951.

Anderson, Paul, and Ken Johnson. **Elk Mountain Odyssey.** Carbondale, 1998.

Aspen Daily Times, Oct. 18, 1890.

Ayers, Mary C. "Howardsville in the San Juans" in *Colorado Magazine,* Summer, 1955.

Baker, Augusta. "The Ute Indians" Unpublished M. A. Thesis, University of Denver, 1926.

Baldwin, Donald. "Wilderness: Concept and Challenge" in *Colorado Magazine*, Summer, 1977.

Ballantyne, Marvin D. Unpublished "Interview with Ed Schmidt" (friend of pilot Walt Piele) Montrose, 1985.

Bancroft, Caroline. **Famous Aspen**. Denver, 1954.

Barcus, Earlynne, and Irma Harrison. **Echoes of a Dream**. Fruita, 1983.

Barret, Golden. "The Surgical Exploits of Dr. W. R. Winters" in Durango D.A.R. **Pioneers of the San Juan Country,** Vol. 1, 1946.

Barrows, Pete, and Judith Holmes. **Colorado's Wildlife Story**. Denver, 1990.

Bender, Henry E. Jr. **Uintah Railway: The Gilsonite Route.** Berkeley, California, 1970.

Bean, Luther. **Once Upon a Time**. Alamosa,, 1975.

Black, Robert C., III. **Island In The Rockies: The Pioneer Era of Grand County,** Colorado. Granby, 1969.

Blankston, Wilma Crisp. **Where Eagles Winter.** Cortez, 1987.

Borland, Lois. "My Friends in High Places" Unpublished manuscript, Western State College, Gunnison, n.d.

Borneman, Walter R. "Black Smoke Among the Clouds." in *Colorado Magazine*, fall, 1975.

Brigham, Lillian Rice. **Colorado Travelore**, Denver, 1938.

Brown, Dee. **Wondrous Times on the Frontier.** New York, N. Y. 1991.

Brown, Robert L. **Holy Cross: The Mountain and the City.** Caldwell, Idaho, 1970.

Brown, William M. "History of the Cebolla-Powderhorn County" Unpublished M.A. Thesis, Western State College, Gunnison, 1935.

Bryce, Mrs. John. "A Lost Cemetery" in Durango D.A.R. **Pioneers of the San Juan Country,** Vol. IV, Durango, 1961.

Burroughs, John Rolphe. **Steamboat in the Rockies.** Fort Collins, 1974.

_____.**Where the Old West Stayed Young.** New York, N.Y., 1962.

Byers, William N. "Ute Legends" in *Out West,* July, 1873.

Cairns, Mary Lyons. **Grand Lake: The Pioneers.** Frederick, (1971) 1991

Campbell, Robert. "The Valley Curtain" *Grand Junction Daily Sentinel,* August 27, 1972.

Campbell, Rosemae Wells. **Crystal River Valley: Jewel or Jinx?** Denver, 1966

Carhart, Arthur. Papers. Denver Public Library.

Carpenter, Farrington. **Confessions of a Maverick.** Denver, 1984

Casebier, Caleb. "The Toughest Game Warden of All" *Colorado Outdoors,* January-February, 1987.

Chevron Oil Company. **Field History, Rangely Weber Sand Unit, Rio Blanco County, Colorado.** Rangely, 1998.

Christo. **Christo: The Valley Curtain, Rifle, Colorado, 1971-1972.** n.p., n.d.

Chronic, Halka. **Roadside Geology of Colorado.** Missoula, Mont. 1980.

Churchill, Richard. **The McCartys: They Rode with Butch Cassidy.** Leadville, 1972.

Colorado Energy Research Institute. **Energy Issues in Colorado's Future.** Colorado School of Mines, Golden, 1980.

Colorado Heritage Magazine. "Follow That Story" Spring, 1988.

Colorado State Planning Commission. **Colorado Yearbook, 1962-4.** Denver, 1964.

Cook, Bruce. **Dalton Trumbo.** New York, N. Y. 1977

Craig Empire, Feb. 22 and 28, 1917.

Cram, George. **Cram's Superior Atlas of Colorado and the World.** Chicago, Ill. 1909.

Crofutt, George A. **Grip Sack Guide of Colorado.** Denver, 1881.

Crum, Josie M. "The Winning of the Spring" in Durango D.A.R. **Pioneers of the San Juan Country,** Vol. I, Durango, 1942.

Cummins, D. H. "Social and Economic History of Southwest Colorado" Unpublished PhD Dissertation, University of Texas, Austin, Texas, 1951.

Davidson, Levette Jay. "Colorado Folklore" in *Colorado Magazine,* Jan.. 1941.

Dawson, Thomas, in **The Trail,** Denver, Sept. 1920.

Delany, Robert. **Blue Coats, Redskins and Black Gowns.** Durango, 1977.

Delta County Independent, April 25, 1940.

Delta Flying Club Scrapbook, Delta County Historical Museum.

Doherty, Debra. **Delta, Colorado: The First 100 Years**. Delta, 1981.

Dolores News, Rico, Jan. 2, 1886.

Eberhart, Perry. **Guide to the Colorado Ghost Towns and Mining Camps**. Denver, 1959.

_____. **Treasure Tales of the Rockies**. Denver, 1961.

Encyclopedia Americana, 1992 edition.

Encyclopedia Britannica, 11th Ed., 1911.

Fairfield, Ula King. "Cultural Expressions in Delta County" in *Colorado Magazine*, Nov. 1946.

Fay, Abbott. **Famous Coloradans**, Paonia, 1990.

_____. **I Never Knew That About Colorado**. Ouray, 1997.

_____. **Mountain Academia**. Boulder, 1968.

_____. **Ski Tracks in the Rockies**. Evergreen, 1984

Federal Writers Project, W.P.A. **Colorado: A Guide to the Highest State**. New York, N.Y., 1941.

Feister, Mark. **Blasted, Beloved Breckenridge**. Boulder, 1973.

Ferrier, Mamie, and George Sibley. **Long Horns and Short Tales: A History of the Crawford Country**. Crawford, 1982; 1983.

Fetter, Richard L. and Suzanne C., **Telluride: From Pick to Powder**. Caldwell, Idaho. 1979.

Fitzpatrick, V.S. **Blue Mountain and Black Midnight**. Craig, 1979.

Foster, Jack. **Adventures at Timberline**. Denver, 1950.

Foutz, Dell R. **Geology of Colorado Illustrated**. Grand Junction, 1994.

Gibbons, Rev. J.J. **In the San Juans: Sketches**. Chicago, Ill., 1898.

Gilliland, Mary Ann. **Frisco: A Colorful Colorado Community**. Frisco, 1984.

_____. **Summit: A Gold Rush History of Summit County, Colorado**. Silverthorne, 1960

Golden, David. "The Rise and Fall of a Small-Town Progressive" in *Journal of the Western Slope*, Summer, 1995.

Grand Junction Daily Sentinel, September 13, 1998.

Grand Valley Gazette, Palisade, May 1974.

Greager, Howard E. **The Hell That Was Paradox**. Boulder, 1992.

Gregory, Marvin, and P. David Smith. **Mountain Mysteries: The Ouray Odyssey**. Ouray, 1984.

Griswold, Don and Jean. **Colorado's Century of "Cities"**. Denver, 1958.

_____. "The Denver, South Park and Pacific Railroad" in **Denver Westerners Brand Book,** 1968.

Gulliford, Andrew. **Boomtown Blues: Colorado's Oil Shale, 1884-1985.** Niwot, 1989.

Gunnison Daily Review, April 28, 1882.

Hanchett, Lafayette. **The Old Sheriff and Other True Tales.** New York, N. Y. 1937.

Harbottle, William. In Carolyn and Clarence Wright: **Tiny Hinsdale of the Silvery San Juan.** Denver, 1954.

Horan, Jame D. **The Authentic West: Accounts by Eyewitnesses and the Outlaws Themselves.** New York, N.Y. 1977.

Haut, Kathy. **Roads to Rangely.** Rangely, 1996.

Hyman, Sidney. **The Aspen Idea.** Norman, Okla. 1975.

Iden, Thomas L. "A History of the Ute Indian Cessions of Colorado." Unpublished M.A. Thesis, Western State College, Gunnison, 1929.

Indian Affairs Office. **Reports, 1849-1990.** Denver Federal Archives Center.

Ingersoll, Earnest. **Knocking Around the Rockies.** New York, N. Y., 1883.

Jack, Ellen. **The Fate of a Fairy.** Chicago, Ill. 1910.

Jackson, W. H. "A Visit to the Los Pinos Agency in 1874" in *Colorado Magazine,* Nov. 1938.

Jessen, Ken. **Colorado Gunsmoke.** Loveland, 1986.

Jocknick, Sidney. **Early Days on the Western Slope of Colorado.** Denver, 1913.

Kania, Alan J. **John Otto: Trials and Trails.** Niwot, 1996.

Knapp, Lena Stark. "Meads Make Pioneer History" in Durango D.A.R. **Pioneers of the San Juan Country,** Vol. II. Durango, 1946.

Knight, McDonald, and Leonard Hammock. **Early Days on the Eagle.** Eagle, 1965.

Larsh, Ed. **Leadville, U.S.A.** Boulder, 1993.

Lavender, David. **One Man's West.** New York, N. Y. 1946.

Leonard, Stephen J. **Trials and Triumphs: A Colorado Portrait of the Great Depression.** Niwot, 1993.

Look, A. **Unforgettable Characters of Western Colorado.** Boulder, 1966.

Lynch, June. "Pagosa! Pagosa! Healing Waters" in Durango D.A.R. **Pioneers of the San Juan Country,** Vol. IV, Durango, 1961.

MacKendrick, Donald A. "Cesspools, Alkalai and White Lily Soap: The Grand Junction Indian School, 1886-1911" in *Journal of the Western Slope,* Summer, 1993.

Marcy, Col. Randolph B. **Thirty Years of Army Life on the Border**. New York, N. Y. 1866.

Marsh, Charles S. **People of the Shining Mountains**. Boulder, 1982.

Marshall, John, and Jerry Roberts. **Living (and Dying) in Avalanche Country**. Silverton, 1992.

Marshall, John B. and Temple, H. Cornelius. **Golden Treasures of the San Juans**. Denver, 1961.

Marshall, Muriel. **Uncompahgre**. Caldwell, Idaho, 1979.

_____. **Where Rivers Meet**. College Station, Texas, 1996.

Marshall, William. Untitled Manuscript. Colorado Historical Society, Denver.

McConnell, Virginia. **Bayou Salado: The Story of South Park**. Denver, 1966.

McCreanor, Emma. **Mesa County, Colorado: A 100 Year History**. Grand Junction, 1986.

McGraw, L. R. (Mac). **Mountain Tales, Faded Tracks and Hi-Jinks**. Gunnison, 1991.

McMechan, A. C. "The Hermit of Pat's Hole" in *Colorado Magazine*, May, 1942.

Meeker Herald. Sept. 10, 1998.

Millich, Arlene A. "A Syllabus For Southern Ute Culture and Traditions." Unpublished Manuscript, Fort Lewis College, Durango, 1976.

Monroe, Arthur. **San Juan Silver**. Montrose, 1940.

Montrose Press, Aug. 10, 1928.

Montroy, Ila. "Colonel C. T. Stollsteimer" in Durango D.A.R. **Pioneers of the San Juan Country,** Vol .IV. Durango, 1961.

Morrell, Jenifer Hanks. "Military Memories of Glen Hanks and the Tenth Mountain Division" in *Journal of the Western Slope*, Winter 1997.

Musser, Eda Baker. **Trails and Trials**. Delta, 1986.

National Geographic Magazine. February, 1918.

Noel, Thomas J., Paul E. Mahoney and Richard E. Stevens. **Historical Atlas of Colorado**. Norman, Okla. 1944.

North Fork Times. Paonia, Dec. 10, 1975.

O'Neal, Bill. **Encyclopedia of Western Gunfighters**. Norman, Okla., 1979.

O'Neal, Floyd, ed. **The Southern Utes: A Tribal History**. Ignacio, 1972.

Ouray Herald, Feb. 24, 1897.

Petite, Jan. **Utes: The Mountain People**. Boulder, 1990.

Rathwell, Ruth. **Of Record and Reminiscence: Ouray and Silverton**. Ouray, 1976.

Rawson, Fred. "Rico's First Religious Service" in Durango D.A.R. **Pioneers of the San Juan Country,** Vol. III. Durango, 1952.

Reyher, Ken. **Antoine Robidoux and Fort Uncompahgre.** Ouray, 1998.

Ripley, Henry and Martha. **Hand-Clasp of the East and West.** Denver, 1914.

Rifle Reading Club. **Rifle Shots.** Rifle, 1973.

Rifle Reveille, Dec. 11, 1902.

Rio Blanco Historical Society, Inc. **This is What I Remember** Vol. I. Meeker, 1972.

Rockwell, Wilson. **Uncompahgre Country.** Denver, 1965.

Rocky Mountain News, Denver, April 29, 1882.

Roeber, Clinton. **West Elk Tales.** Paonia, 1987.

Root, George A. "Gunnison in the Early Eighties" in *Colorado Magazine,* Nov. 1932.

Ruland, Sylvia. **The Lion of Redstone.** Boulder, 1981.

Sammons, Loline. **They Came to Powderhorn**. Gunnison, 1981.

Sanchez, Manuel. "La Posta" in Durango D.A.R. **Pioneers of the San Juan Country,** Vol. VI. Durango, 1961.

Sanfanda, Elizabeth, and Molly L. Med. "The Ladies of French Street in Breckenridge" *Colorado Magazine,* Winter/Spring, 1979.

Shoemaker, Len. **Roaring Fork Valley.** Denver, 1958.

_____. **Saga of a Forest Ranger.** Boulder, 1958.

_____. "The Wheeler Geologic Area and the Passes of the Elk Mountain Range" **Denver Westerners Brand Book, 1968.**

Smith, Anne M. **Ethnology of the Northern Utes.** Albuquerque, N. M. 1974.

Smith, Duane. **In The River of Sorrows: The History of the Lower Dolores River Valley.** USGP Office, Denver, n.d.

_____. **When Coal was King: A History of Crested Butte, Colorado,** 1880-1952. Golden , 1984.

Smith, P. David. **Mountains of Silver.** Boulder, 1994.

Sprague, Marshall. **The Great Gates: The Story of the Rocky Mountain Passes.** Boston, Mass. 1964.

Spurr, Dick and Wendy. **Historic Forts of Colorado.** Grand Junction, 1994.

Starr, John W. "The Crookedest Railroad in the West" *Grand Junction Daily Sentinel,* May 7, 1972.

Stegner, Wallace. **Beyond the Hundredth Meridian**. Boston, Mass. 1954.

Stevenson, Thelma. **Historic Hahn's Peak.** Fort Collins, 1976.

Swanson, Gerald. "Shrine: A Silverton Miracle?" in *Silverton Standard and Miner* vacation guide, 1980.

Telluride Daily Journal, Nov 20, 1903.

Thompson, James B. "Some Redskin Reminiscences" in **The Frontier,** Jan. 1906.

Thompson, Thomas Gray. **Lake City, Colorado: Early Day Social and Cultural History.** Oklahoma City, Okla. 1974.

Towler, Surveva. **The History of Skiing at Steamboat Springs.** Steamboat Springs, 1987.

Tweedle, Robert. "A New Generation of Ghost Towns" in *Denver Post* Aug. 3, 1980.

Urquhart, Lena. **Roll Call: The Violent and Lawless.** Denver, 1967.

Valley Chronicle, Paonia, Feb. 1998.

Vandenbusche, Duane. **The Gunnison Country.** Gunnison, 1988.

Veltri, Myrtle M. and Michele. **The Crested Butte Melting Pot.** Crested Butte, 1986.

Viers, Lawrence and Winona. **Bits and Pieces of Olathe History.** Olathe, 1975

Wallace, Betty. **History With the Hide Off.** Denver, 1965.

Wallihan, Allen G. **Hoofs, Claws and Antlers of the Rocky Mountains by Camera.** Denver, 1902.

_____. "Photographing Wild Life in Early Colorado" *Colorado Magazine,* Sept. 1944.

Wardrip, Molly K. **A History of Montezuma County**, Colorado. Mancos, 1958.

_____. **Montezuma's Trails of Time.** Cortez, 1993.

Wegner, Martin G. **Recollections of Telluride, Colorado, 1895-1920.** Grand Junction, 1978.

Western Colorado Power Company Records. Fort Lewis College, Durango.

Wirth, Kelsey. **Reflections on a Western Town: An Oral History of Crested Butte, Colorado.** Crested Butte, 1996.

Wolcott, Frank H. "Monarch of Grand County" **Denver Westerners Brand Book, 1954.**

Wolle, Muriel Sibell. **Stampede to Timberline.** Boulder, 1949.

Yaskoweak, Marci. **Land Dancing: A History of the Starr Nelson Ranch,** Delta, 1995.

Young, Leslie. "Colorado's Best Known Ranch Women" *Frontier Magazine,* Craig, Aug. 1998.

INDEX